If you've ever parented a child in crisis, you're in good company—Stacy Lee Flury serves as a voice of compassion and wisdom after spending years in the trenches with her own daughter. Now, she's able to offer comfort, encouragement, and the practical advice she gleaned from walking through her own "valley of the shadow."

Jim Daly
President—Focus on the Family

Stacy Lee's vulnerability and transparency in her writing is so relatable that it deeply touches the hearts of her readers, especially those who have experienced the emotions associated with being a parent of a wayward child. She not only shares from her own painful struggles of raising a difficult teen, but she offers hope by pointing to the promises of Jesus as she talks about how He lifted her out of the pit of despair and began to heal her. This book will be both uplifting and encouraging to anyone who reads it.

Cathy Taylor
Founder of *Hurting Moms, Mending Hearts*—A community of hurting moms, with teens/young adults in crisis, connecting to find hope, healing and restoration. www.hurtingmoms.com

If your heart is breaking over your young person, please read *Turning the Tide of Emotional Turbulence*. Stacy's humility and self-disclosure will help prevent the self-blame that haunts us parents. Her testimony of God's provision will encourage you to keep walking one more day. Her answers, forged in the fires of raw pain, are not shallow or simplistic—they are valuable counsel. The chapter on blame alone is worth whatever you pay for this book.

Lynne Babbitt
Psychotherapist at Lynne Babbitt Counseling and mother of six (now grown) teenagers and foster parent of 23 children
www.lynnebabbitt.com

Stacy Flury authentically shares personal stories from her own journey with a troubled daughter. I walked with Stacy through part of her parenting struggles and I know her heart's desire for this book is to help others on a similar path. These devotionals are full of relevant spiritual truths hurting moms and dads need to hear. Readers will enjoy her easy-to-read format with practical insights on a variety of topics including application questions and prayers to pray. Thank you, Stacy, for persevering through endless trials so that you could offer this gift to parents with broken hearts.

Dena Yohe

Co-founder of *Hope for Hurting Parents*, mentor, speaker, and award-winning author of *You Are Not Alone: Hope for Hurting Parents of Troubled Kids*

Without a doubt, as you read Stacy Lee Flury's devotional you will find it to be one of the best available for parents in today's world of troubled teens. As her pastor I have personally witnessed many of the challenges she faced in faith, bold resolve and unwavering determination. On the surface I thought I saw a little boat tossed about in a turbulent storm when all the while it turned out to be a huge ocean liner steady on her course! Thoughtful, insightful and compassionate, *Turning the Tide of Emotional Turbulence* will become a resourceful and handy companion to every parent looking for answers from God's Word. This magnificent devotional helps the reader prayerfully sort through thoughts and emotions before they become hopelessly overwhelming. As you journey through its pages, Stacy Lee will take you to the heart of God where honest answers can be found for both the parent and the troubled teen. Written without pretense or platitudes, this excellent devotional will deeply minister to your heart every day. Every parent who can relate to Stacy Lee's struggles will find this devotional to be a spiritual oasis. *Turning the Tide of Emotional Turbulence* might very well be considered a notable benchmark by which all devotionals can be measured.

Pastor Bill Brendel
Glad Tidings Assembly of God Church, Mt. Ephraim, NJ

Stacy Lee Flury speaks with a true, honest, and authentic voice in *Turning the Tide of Emotional Turbulence.* Any parent who has ever raised a teenager will relate to the challenges of this stage of life, but especially those who have experienced the despair and pain of life with a teen in crisis. Stacy's willingness to open her heart and tell the story of her family will give other parents hope in the midst of their difficult situation. It is only through the Anchor that is Jesus Christ that these struggles can be faced, and it is possible to walk this painful journey with Him by your side. Stacy's story offers words of hope, encouragement, and wisdom for any parent who feels abandoned and alone. *Turning the Tide of Emotional Turbulence* is Stacy's story of the power of prayer and trusting God in the depths of crisis, and it can also be the story of every parent who has ever walked this painful pathway, with faith in the Anchor of our soul, Jesus Christ.

Nina Newton
Sr. Editor, *RUBY Magazine*: Your Voice, Your Story

Turning the Tide of
EMOTIONAL
TURBULENCE

Devotions for Parents
with Teens in Crisis

by Stacy Lee Flury

Pageant Wagon Publishing
Vineland, New Jersey

Turning the Tide of Emotional Turbulence:
Devotions for Parents with Teens in Crisis

By Stacy Lee Flury © 2019

ISBN: 978-0-9981771-9-9

Imprint Pageant Wagon Publishing
A Division of Pageant Wagon Productions LLC
Layout, Design, and Edited by Kathryn Ross
www.pageantwagonpublishing.com
info@pageantwagonpublishing.com

Cover Photography by Ruth Nyce, https://ruthnyce.wixsite.com/homepage/

Bible versions throughout this book are copyrighted by the following:

Table of Contents

Dedication

This book is dedicated to all parents who struggle
with a teen or young adult in crisis.

"It is good for me to have
been afflicted,
that I might know how
to speak a word in season
to one that is weary."

— Charles Spurgeon

Whether your child is suffering with addiction, disorders, mental
illness, or a multitude of other issues, you are not alone as you
face the emotional storms of your journey. This devotional is
meant for you.

From one parent to another, please know this: God loves you and
your child. My prayer is that you find hope, comfort, and healing
through the words and personal experiences I've shared in this
book. May God be your help to turn the tide of emotional
turbulence in your life.

Introduction

My Story

My parenting fantasies of raising a perfect little family through deliriously happy milestones of life crashed on the shoreline of reality. As my children entered their teens, turbulent storms stirred the current of our home life, washing over us in a tempest of unanticipated trials and emotions. Peace receded out of reach like the undertow of a riptide.

Drenched in waves of turmoil, I wondered how such a thing could happen. My prayer list did not include unrest and upheaval. After all, who stands in line asking God for an ocean of heartache? I didn't expect it, nor did I ever expect to write a book about it, exposing struggles, failures, and disappointments weathered, for all the world to read.

But God had other plans.

I've often asked Him, "Why did You choose us to parent a struggling and hurting teen?" Not that I questioned if God knew what He was doing, but more how He would use our painful circumstances to honor His name.

As the years passed, my eyes opened fully to see the hurt and brokenness in our family. My husband suffered several strokes and a bout of severe psoriasis due to stress. I dropped to a weight of 95 pounds, fallen into the deep, dark canyon of depression. Both our teens struggled through this time—all of us shattered in some way.

The hard truth of our situation sharpened in focus when our youngest daughter manifested an increasing number of serious problems. She wrestled with abandonment, depression, identity issues, suicidal tendencies, low self-esteem, and body image obsessions, as well as a leaning towards self-harm. Doctors diagnosed her with a processing disorder, Post-Traumatic Stress Disorder, mild mood-disorder, anxiety, and short-term memory issues. She experimented with drugs which very nearly took her life. Unhealthy relationships with others victimized her through mental and emotional abuse. Being adopted also brought many challenges. The list continued with a plethora of other troubles adding to the cyclone of her life.

I searched exhaustively for answers while growing my skills in hiding shame, embarrassment, and guilt. I didn't want others to know the severity of our broken family and how my husband and I felt like failed parents. Adrift, alone—so alone—I couldn't find anyone else struggling like me. I feared to trust others with my pain, wishing instead for a magic wand to make it all go away.

Waves of trials and troubles beat us over and over with no relief. To stay afloat, we hung onto the only life preserver we knew—our Lord and Savior, Jesus Christ—our Anchor in the storms of life.

God, in His wisdom and love, did not make our difficulties go away. Instead, he called us to plunge deeper where

He could reveal Himself and deliver us from the things in our lives that did not belong there. He wanted us to survive and rise out of the depths of crises to become a beacon of hope for others who struggled on the stormy seas and rocky jetties of life.

Once His Light exposed the true nature of our issues, we journeyed forward into healing and redemption. It was not overnight. It took time. It took patience. It took endurance. It took counsel, resources, and the help of others. Though an overwhelming process at times, our Anchor in the storms proved sure and faithful.

Today, we continue to learn and grow, imperfect still, navigating the daily challenge to be accountable and responsible parents. We make many mistakes along the way. All parents do. My husband once teased, "I really hate those parents over there. They have perfect kids." We know now that playing the comparison game proves useless to healing. Instead, we trust God to give correction when needed, and forgiveness when we repent. Every day is a challenge, but when we rely on Him, He carries us through every fierce storm we chance to encounter.

Without the help of God, family, and close friends, we would not have made it through our darkest days. Prayers, journal writing, therapy, a shoulder to cry on, or a buddy to console with, kept us from losing our hope. There are support groups, resources, and counselors to help, but there is only ONE GOD who knows and understands the exact nature of the trials that confront us, and the way of deliverance in the fray. Surely, He has a good plan for us.

Isaiah 55:8 NASB says: *"For My thoughts are not your thoughts, nor are your ways My ways," declares the LORD.*

Our limited minds cannot comprehend God's plans, but I trust they are for good as it says in Jeremiah 29:11-13 NASB: *"For I know the plans that I have for you," declares the LORD, "plans for welfare and not for calamity to give you a future and a hope. Then you will call upon Me and come and pray to Me, and I will listen to you. You will seek Me and find Me when you search for Me with all your heart."*

How to Use this Devotional

Throughout this book I use my daughter Daniela's real name while keeping certain details private. She joins me in prayer for you that your hope and faith may increase as God intervenes and rescues your child, in the same way He reached down and lifted Daniela out of the swirling depths. God is faithful. Today, my daughter is rescued, married, and raising a family of her own with her husband, Edwin. They have two beautiful children, Malia and Isaac.

Each chapter in this book is designed as a weekly devotional, intended to settle the waves of highly charged emotions we, as parents, experience when walking with our teen or young adult in crisis. The readings refocus our mind and heart on the One who provides us with the answers and guidance we need: our Heavenly Father.

The alphabetized Table of Contents help you find your way through specific emotions or struggles each week. Personal experience stories, challenge questions, and a place to journal thoughts and vent feelings combine with prayer and extra Scriptures at the end of each chapter. Incorporate them into your devotions for the week.

I pray this book brings clarity and wisdom to you, surviving the trials of parenting through turbulent waters. Whether you hop around from one emotion-specific chapter to the other or start from the very beginning and work your way through, God will meet you there.

May you find encouragement and biblical truth through my story, confident of this truth: You are not alone. Christ is your Anchor to help you survive your parenting storms. I join my prayers with yours!

Stacy Lee Flury
July 2019

"God doesn't want us
to rescue our children.
He's the Rescuer."

— Elizabeth Musser

ABANDONMENT

Arouse Yourself, why do You sleep, O Lord?
Awake, do not reject us forever.
Why do You hide Your face and forget our
affliction and our oppression?
Psalm 44:23-24 NASB

I cried, I begged, I sought, and I asked to no avail. An enormous chasm of abandonment engulfed me. I felt like God didn't care to answer me in my troubles. The Psalmist echoes this feeling when he cries out in Psalm 44:24 NASB, *"Why do You hide Your face and forget our affliction and our oppression?"*

Silence from Heaven. Total and eerie silence.

Do you feel rejected and abandoned? Perhaps you shake your head in confusion. "Does God not care about me and my family? Does He not want our broken family restored?" Many parents have wondered these things when dire circumstances in their lives linger unchanged.

I've often wondered if my problems just weren't critical enough for God to intervene. Why had my situation remained the same? Why was I unmoved from the seat of disappointment and despair?

Daniela craved suicide as a cure for her pain. Her anger expanded to include a willingness to hurt others besides herself. Daniela's issues grew deeper and more painful for us, as parents, to address. I sat, before God, with no answers forthcoming to give me hope of deliverance.

I felt abandoned.

I wasn't the only one who ever felt this way. King David reveals in the Psalms how often he felt abandoned, too, for any number of reasons. Enemies sought to kill him. His children rebelled and betrayed him. Consider his words in Psalm 13:1-2 NASB, *"How long, O LORD? Will you forget me forever? How long will you hide your face from me? How long must I wrestle with my thoughts and day after day have sorrow in my heart?"*

In the days when I felt abandoned, I continued to cry out to God. To beg. To seek. To ask. At the end of myself, there was nothing else to do—unless I gave up all hope. Heaven seemed silent, and God far from my broken heart.

Until one day, in prayer, He made known to me that He was near. Very near. God did hear me! He saw my anguish. He knew the depths of my abandonment. I did not have to tell Him the intensity of my agony. He already knew!

I should have known. It is the pattern of the Psalms. Anguish. A sense of abandonment. Then, God shows Himself near.

At the end of Psalm 13, David praises and rejoices in the Lord: *"But I trust in your unfailing love; my heart rejoices in your salvation. I will sing the LORD's praise, for he has been good to me."* v. 5-6 NIV. David's expression of faithfulness to God, even in the midst of his perceived emotional abandonment, finds eventual satisfaction in God's response. He never stopped listening or caring for David in his woes.

He never stops listening or caring for me in my woes. If I believed otherwise, it would be a lie from the enemy.

In the empty moments, David learned something vital: His most difficult circumstances in life were his most intimate times with God. He discovered how to be thankful in all situations, even in those seasons where he thought God did not hear him.

In our sense of abandonment, it may appear that God tarries at a distance. In truth, He is often closer than we think.

God does all things for a reason and in due season. He always works on our behalf. In fact, God loves to display His grace and mercy towards us in the midst of the most turbulent storms we may encounter. He just answers them in a different way than what we expect.

I asked God to help my daughter through the stormy waves that threatened to drown her. I pleaded with Him, surrendering to Him—do whatever is necessary to rescue her and our family in crisis. I felt as if my words bounced off the walls and ceiling in a hollow room.

But six months later, God's answer arrived with more than I had asked for. He sent the Storm Patrol with provision and healing through the counselors and prayer partners that I needed for Daniela. As well as myself.

It's sometimes hard to accept, but God calls us to patience. He wants us to remain faithful and praise Him in the midst of our crisis. We draw close to Him in spirit when we pray and meditate on His Word. Patience, waiting on Him in faith, replaces the sense of emotional abandonment when crisis doesn't correct on our timeline. His appointed timing is perfect. Always.

Trust God. He's been with you. He will continue to be with you. He loves you. He will not forsake you.

Go Deeper

 What are some examples in your life of feeling abandoned?

 What are some ways in which God has expressed to you that He hears and cares about you?

 Write out Deuteronomy 3:18 and post to your mirror or wall to remind you every day that God has not forgotten or forsaken you.

Meditate on Scripture

I will never desert you, nor will I ever forsake you.

Hebrews 13:5 NASB

Turn to me and be gracious to me, For I am lonely and afflicted. The troubles of my heart are enlarged; Bring me out of my distresses.

Psalm 25:16-17 NIV

For God says, "At just the right time, I heard you. On the day of salvation, I helped you." Indeed, the "right time" is now. Today is the day of salvation.

2 Corinthians 6:2 NLT

Pray

Dear Heavenly Father,

Thank you for being so faithful in my journey as a parent. I will trust you when I feel forgotten by You. Turn to me and be gracious, for I am lonely and afflicted. The troubles of my heart are enlarged; bring me out of my distresses. Show me Lord, how to lean on Your Word for the hope and comfort I need. I will praise You no matter how bleak or overwhelming the circumstances are around me, for I know you will never forsake me. Increase my patience so I can learn how to rely on You when I cannot visibly see the changes I long for. Thank you for always being by my side, encouraging me to trust You at all times. You have heard me and helped me when I called out to You for salvation.

Amen

"Sometimes you must
stand still
in order to get moving
to where God
wants you to go."

— D.A. McBride

ANGER

In your anger do not sin:
Do not let the sun go down while you are still angry,
and do not give the devil a foothold.
Ephesians 4:26 NIV

Shoved deep in the crevices of my being, a gush of anger churned, about to blow like the Old Faithful geyser in Yellowstone National Park. I dared not exhibit my rage in order to keep Daniela's depression and abandonment issues at bay. Each day I'd retire to bed wondering if I should ask God's forgiveness in my anger. I wasn't sure if it was necessary since I felt justified in harboring it.

I never fully understood how much anger I kept locked inside until one day when Daniela asked, "Do you hate me? Are you angry at me?"

"No," I blurted in shocked response. "I love you!"

But my words rang hollow in her ears. Daniela perceived my deep-seated anger, interpreting it as a lack of love for her. As crisis episodes increased, rising like storm tossed waves in the ocean, my stress levels elevated. Daniela's extreme and destructive behaviors left me boggled in mind, drained in spirit, and frustrated in hope.

Due to multiple unresolved problems—not just from Daniela, but other sources, too—anger remained pent up inside me. These stress fractures exacerbated anger symptoms such as clenching my teeth at night while I slept. I could not allow my pent-up anger to burst forth or I'd be seen as an appalling Christian and terrible mother.

What was all this anger? I made a list:

- I was angry at others who regarded me as a bad parent because of what my teen did.
- I was angry that I must parent a teen in perpetual crisis instead of a normal teen.
- I was angry at families who posted how blessed they were across social media.
- I was angry at being tired all the time and not able to find rest and joy like other parents.

Truth be told, I was angry at myself.

My anger grew as I delayed my response in securing outside help for Daniela. The situation did not improve on its own. I remained in denial of her serious troubles, even when she implored me for help. This added more agony to her woes.

Rather than face the reality of our situation head on, I quenched truth, which turned to a covert rage within me. I put my pride before her welfare and justified my selfishness, excusing the sin of anger. This swept me into a never-ending whirlpool—a vicious cycle leading to more sin, and ultimately, a barrier between me and God.

Anger ruled my life, robbed of God's peace. The Lord could not be glorified by my inner fury. I'd given the devil more than a foothold. I gave him a doorway into my very heart.

I know I'm not the only one who has entertained anger. In Genesis 4, Cain's heart was not right before God. He killed his brother out of anger. In Numbers 20, Moses was angry at the people of God for all their complaining and mumbling and lost his patience. In order to secure water for the people, he struck a rock twice when God specifically instructed him to simply speak to the rock. In the end, Moses paid dearly for his actions.

Doctors warn that harboring unresolved anger is a leading cause of health problems such as stroke, depression, ulcers, high blood pressure, and in my case, grinding of the teeth. No wonder God's Word tells us to not let the sun go down on our anger.

When I could handle the churning waves of my rage no longer, I finally realized the depth of my sin. For too long I'd held fast to the anger in my heart stemming from how my daughter's troubles impacted me. I knew I must repent and ask forgiveness from her. It stung to admit that I'd not been the parent God called me to be. I needed her to know I was wrong for embracing an angry attitude. Only through my confession to God, seeking His mercy, forgiveness, and direction, could I expect to see my anger turn around, so healing might begin.

That day, I woke as a parent. With humility and gratitude to God for revealing the truth to my heart, I chose to move forward with a new mindset.

Anger is an emotional tool Satan uses to deceive and tear both us and our teens down. We must not let anger control us. Instead, we must admit and submit our anger to God. When we recognize the spirit of anger as sin, we stop the enemy in his tracks.

Ask God's forgiveness. Receive His mercy and healing. In so doing, God crushes the enemy's hold on you and restores freedom to your life.

Go Deeper

 Do you have an attitude of anger towards others, difficult circumstances, or even God? What must you do to be delivered from the control of anger?

There is righteous anger and unrighteous anger. Do you know the difference through these Scriptures? 1 Kings 11:9-10 and Genesis 4:5-8. Which of the two do you see as a reflection of yourself?

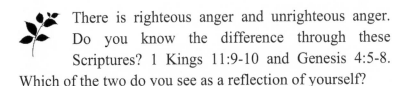 Has there been a time when you have been angry at your teen for his/her problems? If so, God wants to loosen you from the stranglehold of anger. Read Ephesians 4:31-32; Proverbs 14:29; and 1 Corinthians 13:4-5. Ask God to heal you so that compassion rises above anger.

Meditate on Scripture

Get rid of all bitterness, rage and anger, brawling and slander, along with every form of malice. Be kind and compassionate to one another, forgiving each other, just as in Christ God forgave you.

Ephesians 4:31-32 NIV

Refrain from anger and turn from wrath; do not fret - it leads only to evil.

Psalm 37:8 NIV

May these words of my mouth and this meditation of my heart be pleasing in your sight, LORD, my Rock and my Redeemer.

Psalm 19:14 NIV

My dear brothers and sisters, take note of this: Everyone should be quick to listen, slow to speak and slow to become angry, because human anger does not produce the righteousness that God desires.

James 1:19-20 NIV

Pray

Dear Heavenly Father,

I mourn to realize that I've let selfish anger control my attitude and seep into my heart. I've been foolish in my decisions and have hindered what You, Lord, were trying to show me. Help me to rid my heart of all bitterness, fury, and anger in every form. Remove thoughts of rage from my mind. Replace them with compassion, understanding, and patience. Encourage me to listen carefully and use words that bring honor to You when I speak to others. Let me extend forgiveness to others, as You have forgiven me. Let the words and meditations of my heart be always acceptable and pleasing before You. May I not be led by my flesh but by Your Spirit. Let my actions represent my Christian walk and Your unconditional love, especially towards my hurting teen.

Amen

ANXIETY

When anxiety was great within me,
your consolation brought me joy.
Psalm 94:19 NIV

I rushed into the emergency room frantic to find Daniela. Only minutes earlier she'd arrived by ambulance and I'd been given no immediate answers as to her condition. Panic-stricken, I paced in the waiting room. My brain raced in a jumble of torturous thoughts. At one point I felt as if my heart might jump out of me. I didn't want to be here. I feared the worst.

Too nervous to sit, I walked to the front desk again and tried to calmly ask if someone could tell me something. Anything. A kind nurse acknowledged my anxiety and told me he'd check for an update. Finally! At least this was some small help to ease my panicked state of mind. A temporary peace while I waited for more information.

The nurse soon returned to say that the doctors were with her and they'd call for me when they were ready. Not wanting to sit down while I waited, I surveyed the crowded emergency room struck with a sudden thought: *How many of these families were here for the same reason as myself?*

The minute hand on the clock ticked away. But I felt like time stood still, like a clockwork gear stuck in position, unable to move forward. Again, I went to the front desk. Agitated, with a gripping tightness in my chest, I asked, "Can you please let me know what is going on and why I can't go back to see my daughter?"

Earlier that day I'd received a call from a boyfriend of my daughter's that she was sick and I needed to come right away. By the time I arrived, I found her horizontal on the floor, barely conscious—like a crime scene in a movie. White as a ghost and in a zombie state, she could hardly speak, but she could hear me, though she didn't know who I was. In barely audible words she muttered, "I don't want to die."

I glanced about the room and asked a few questions to the others nearby. Laced drugs, it appeared, had been the life-threatening culprit.

Paramedics arrived. They took her vitals. Their facial expressions revealed the critical nature of her condition. The police officer in the room sensed my fear and anxiety. He graciously offered to show me the way to the hospital.

Minutes passed ever so slowly in the waiting room. I petitioned God to calm my racing heart. Thoughts of death tormented me. I forced them away through prayer, whispering quietly under my breath to the God who knew I needed assistance in that instant—and for whatever was to come.

The nurse appeared again and motioned for me to enter by a side door. He pointed out the directions to Daniela's room. I tried to remember what he said as I navigated the hospital halls turning here, then there, like a maze in a cornfield. I prayed I wouldn't get lost until I found the room.

Holding my breath, I parted the curtain to see my little girl lying in a hospital bed like Sleeping Beauty. I took her small, clammy hand in mine and thanked the Lord she was still alive. I was not prepared for this crisis, nor did I ever want to go through it again. Even so, in that moment hovering over my daughter who had come so close to death, God filled me with an unspeakable joy.

She was alive!

When we have a teen battling multiple issues and daily crises, anxiety shadows our mind and heart like a close companion. We always worry about what might happen next and obsess wondering if they are safe. We hover over them and want to tie them down hoping to protect them from their poor choices and decisions.

What can you do to have peace in the midst of that kind of heightened anxiety? Here's a checklist I've learned from experience:

- Carry your Bible with you everywhere you go to read the Word for encouragement and calm your anxious thoughts.
- Post scriptures in your home, car, and workplace to remind you that God is in control.

- Surround yourself with uplifting worship music to relax your emotions and feed your spirit.
- Take long walks to release some of those pent-up thoughts and emotions.
- Vent or talk to a close and trustworthy friend/family member as a listening ear or as someone to pray with you.

Anxiety accompanies crisis. However, God provides the exact portions of strength and faith through your crisis to help you say goodbye to anxiety and hello to peace.

Go Deeper

 Anxiety and fear go together like wind in a storm. As you face your teen's crisis head on, name some things you are anxious about and how God responds when you call on Him?

 In 2 Chronicles 20, we read that King Jehoshaphat loved and obeyed God. His Kingdom was attacked by surprise and he was not prepared. He told his people and small army to be brave when he was very anxious. He prayed, taking control of his thoughts, and centered his mind on what God had done for him in the past. Write down all the things God has done for you in the past when you were anxious and fearful.

 List three ways God shows He is near and present even now in your time of crisis.

Meditate on Scripture

Cast all your anxiety on him because he cares for you.

1 Peter 5:7 NIV

Do not be anxious about anything, but in every situation, by prayer and petition, with thanksgiving, present your requests to God.

Philippians 4:6 NIV

You will keep in perfect peace those whose minds are steadfast, because they trust in you.

Isaiah 26:3 NIV

Pray

Dear Heavenly Father,

When I am confronted with life's challenges, stress and worry, help me cast all my anxiety on You, for I know You care for me. You gave the people of Israel rest—a promise then as it is for me now. Your promises never fail. Let me not be anxious in any situation. Instead, may I consult You and seek Your peace in my circumstances for You ARE peace. Remind me not to get caught up in the *what ifs*, and *should haves*, or worry about what tomorrow will bring. Guard my heart when I don't understand. Sustain me so I may be unshakeable when storms come. I present my requests to You with a heart of gratitude because You are my burden bearer.

Amen

"The beginning of anxiety
is the end of faith,
and the beginning of
true faith
is the end of anxiety."

— George Mueller

ATTITUDE

Whatever happens, conduct yourselves in a manner
worthy of the gospel of Christ.
Philippians 1:27a NIV

Have you ever lost your temper, said the wrong things, or reacted in an immature way in response to someone else? I can tell you with all honesty that I have—and too many times to count. I've also murmured and complained and behaved miserably in situations where I ought to have chosen a more noble response.

If your daily routine includes any of these activities, you may be battling the same nasty habit I wrestle with: A bad attitude.

Let's face it, teens and young adults often drive us crazy. They scare us. They worry us. They put themselves in life altering predicaments that push every button we have, even buttons we didn't know we had.

In such times, how many of us actually stop in the middle of distressing moments and pray? I can be honest— I know I haven't done so, even though I know better.

Have you ever asked for God's wisdom and counsel in how you should respond to a troubling situation? In all truth, I know I often don't. But I've had to change my ways many times.

Teens pick up on our attitudes and sense what our next move, mood, and step might be. I remember yelling at my older daughter BJ, over something that had agitated me. She, in return, yelled back with a threat if I dared to continue. I laughed at her in disbelief. That didn't soften the argument. In fact, my hot temper escalated things like warm ocean waters whip a tropical depression into a hurricane.

If my response to my daughter's sass had been different, I might have subdued the matter. Unfortunately, I reacted without thinking, giving myself over to a negative and cynical attitude. I missed the opportunity to recognize my power to defuse the situation. My lack of self-awareness precipitated the inevitable meltdown between mother and daughter.

After that particular conflict, I thought a good deal about my attitude, concluding that I really wasn't behaving much better than my daughter. What kind of an example did I model for her? How much of my attitude gave glory and honor to Jesus Christ?

In fact, my attitude stunk like a rotten egg. I complained to God about how my kids didn't respect me or appreciate me. I complained about friends hurting me or leaving me. I even complained to God about how I felt stuck with children who gave me a lot of grief.

Life is rough with a child in crisis. For every external outburst, breakdown, tearful, or angry response from our teen, there is an interior, unseen instigator stirring trouble in their heart and confusing their minds, that has yet to be revealed or resolved. As parents, our attitudes can impact those battles for better or worse.

As I pondered these things, I knew I must be on God's side of this battle, bridging the gap, instead widening the continental divide between myself and my children. I prayed for insight and my answer arrived with swift illumination in my mind and heart: I needed a major spiritual overhaul of my attitude.

Changing our self-attitude to a Christ-like attitude is like a marathon. On the starting line, thank God in all things and at all times instead of complaining or indifference. When we choose to respond to every moment with a grateful heart, God's Word affirms that we snuff out any semblance of a bad attitude and create a more Christ-like attitude in its place.

Philippians 4:8b says to fix our thoughts on what is true, honorable, right, pure, lovely, and admirable. As I practiced this, I settled into a calm and peaceful place, fortified with positivity despite being in the midst of a storm—or a very, very long marathon that feels like it may never end.

Even so, God commands us to continually praise Him with our hearts and with our hands lifted high, surrendering our will and our fleshly attitudes so we can be more like Him. Storms diminish. Finish lines loom ahead on the horizon.

What attitude will you carry with you today?

Go Deeper

 What are some attitudes that you struggle with? Does your attitude get in the way of what the Lord wants to do in your own heart and life?

For every negative thought that proceeds from your mouth, say or do something positive that glorifies God and blesses your family. Challenge yourself to see how long you can continue this exercise before it becomes your natural response in every situation.

Meditate on Scripture

And whatever you do, in word or deed, do everything in the name of the Lord Jesus, giving thanks to God the Father through him.

Colossians 3:17 ESV

That, in reference to your former manner of life, you lay aside the old self, which is being corrupted in accordance with the lusts of deceit, and that you be renewed in the spirit of your mind, and put on the new self, which in the likeness of God has been created in righteousness and holiness of the truth.

Ephesians 4:22-24 NASB

In the same way, let your light shine before others, that they may see your good deeds and glorify your Father in heaven.

Matthew 5:16 NIV

Pray

Dear Heavenly Father,

My attitude needs a Godly adjustment. Whatever I say or do, let it give honor to You. Lord, equip me with the tools I need to make attitude changes. Transform my negative attitude to a Godly one so I can experience peace and blessing in my home. Help my attitude to be one of humility, regarding another's interest as much as my own. Teach my spirit and mind to lay aside my old ways and put on the new self in Christlikeness. Let my attitude reflect more of You so I shine before others with holiness and truth. May I be an encouragement to my teen as they deal with their own attitudes. Be glorified Lord, through my new attitude.

Amen

"I've discovered an astonishing truth: God is attracted to weaknesses. He can't resist those who humbly and honestly admit how desperately they need Him."

— Jim Cymbala

BLAME

*Why do you see the speck that is in your brother's eye, but
do not notice the log that is in you*
Matthew 7:3 ESV

Every household keeps this game on the shelf. Some homes
play it more than others. There are no age restrictions.
There are no winners. Only losers. It is not a fun game. In
truth, it destroys relationships and marriages, creating an
environment of negativity and conflict. You know it by its
common name: The Blame Game.

We often played the Blame Game in our house. It
had few rules and involved parents rolling the dice of
whatever contentious issue might come up related to
destructive choices and decisions committed by a child or
teen in crisis living in the home.

For example, roll the dice one day, and the husband
blames the wife for being an enabler. Spin the spinner on
her turn, and the wife blames the husband for not being
man enough to set boundaries and be the disciplinarian.

The Blame Game leads parents through chutes-and-
ladders arguments over who is more-right than the other.
Nothing gets resolved. There is little strategy to the game,

only the continuous gathering of Unrest Tokens and Conflict Cards. The one who collects the most loses. Every time. Never ending.

I played the Blame Game daily with my husband. With champion flair, I focused on his mistakes and faults to distract me from my own transgressions. My knack for finger-pointing added to my losses. I painfully learned the truth in the old adage: When we point our finger at others, three fingers on that same hand point straight back at us.

Blaming others is easy, often a first response when conflict arises. But, like the ripple effect on a smooth surface of water when a stone of contention drops, blame swells into larger, disruptive consequences. Cause to effect.

In truth, I didn't want to take ownership of problems, swirling like turbulent, rippling waters, in the heart and mind of my teen in crisis. To do so required me to confront a guilt buried deep inside of me that I didn't want to face. A roll of the dice or spin of the spinner allowed me to lay blame on someone else.

But the weight of my gathered losses of Blame Game tokens and cards forced me to ask myself the much-avoided Challenge Question: *How often do you work on taking the hefty log out of your eye before you try to remove the speck out of your teen or husband's eyes?*

In my conversations with other parents, I learned that they too, had drawn this very Challenge Question, and struggled with how they would answer it. As we shared our common experiences with the Blame Game, we made a list of some Blame Game starters that drew us into a losing match: I blame you because . . .

- You never disciplined our child when they were younger and now it is too late.
- You let him/her get away with so much and never set a boundary.
- You didn't step into your place as the spiritual leader in our family.
- You could have done more to protect them from getting so deep into trouble.
- You were prideful and never allowed counseling-- that's why our child is like this.
- You never want to deal with the elephant in the room of our troubled teen.
- You repeat the same pattern as our child and that's why they won't change.

Who else do we blame? Ourselves. We add a tremendous amount of guilt and condemnation over our head and believe we deserve this. I blamed myself for enabling some of Daniela's behavior even though she was old enough to make her own choices. I wallowed in guilt for not getting her to counseling early enough despite the fact that she absolutely refused to speak to anyone when we did have an appointment. I condemned myself for a lot of her problems which were not mine to begin with but thought I should take them on because I was her parent.

All this blame did not change our circumstances. In fact, it created more problems. We were left with only one alternative: change how we play the game. Like the legendary King Arthur and the Knights of the Round Table, our kitchen table was the place to congregate and communicate for nobler purposes. It was time to play a new game, so new rules were set in order:

- Begin with prayer.
- No words of disrespect to each other are allowed. Yelling, cursing, or bashing remarks towards one another will not be tolerated.
- Everyone gets a turn to speak.
- Any ideas or a suggestion for a new way of doing things must be handwritten and presented.
- Anything shared at the table--and only at the table-- will not be used as a punishable offense.
- Agreements made at table must be written down and signed by all parties.
- You can disagree but must demonstrate a clear reason for the disagreement and show a willingness to find and work towards solution.
- Evidence and proof of facts must corroborate allegations.
- If a compromise cannot be reached, a third-party mediator may be allowed to assist so long as all parties agree.
- Parents MUST tell the teen that their thoughts ARE valued and that they are loved and respected.
- Thank everyone for their willingness to communicate at the table.
- End with prayer.

After a few meetings we mastered the rules. With

persistence and a few revisions along the way, everyone grew through the process without gaining any Blame Game Tokens. Those game pieces were no longer allowed.

My husband and I chose to talk and forgive each other privately. We owned our sin, mistakes, and poor choices that we'd used to wound each other, and ourselves and became a united front to help our troubled teen.

Satan deceives us into thinking we need to carry the burden of blame on ourselves and foist it upon the backs of others forever. But Christ says, "NO!" Jesus carried our guilt, blame, and condemnation to the Cross, removing that log from our lives forever. We are free. We see clearly. We are empowered to minister freedom to our teen in crisis.

Do you play the Blame Game? Repent. That's the only way to win. Ask God to take the log out of your eye. Seek forgiveness from Him and your family. The next time the Blame Game tries to draw you in, like a strong current pulling you under stormy waters, cry out to God for rescue. He is your anchor, firm and strong. God doesn't play games and He will never let you go.

Go Deeper

 How many times have you played the Blame Game this week? What can you do differently to get rid of the Blame Game for good?

 Read Genesis 3:12-24—Who started the Blame Game in this story and what was the end result? What can we learn from this story?

Meditate on Scripture

You, therefore, have no excuse, you who pass judgment on someone else, for at whatever point you judge another, you are condemning yourself, because you who pass judgment do the same things.

Romans 2:1 NIV

All a man's ways seem right to him, but the LORD evaluates the motives.

Proverbs 21:2 HCSB

So then, each of us will give an account of ourselves to God.

Romans 14:12 NIV

Pray

Dear Heavenly Father,

Forgive me, Lord, for choosing to point my finger at others rather than acknowledge sin in my own life. It is not my place to pass judgment. When I do, I know I'm only condemning myself for the same things. Examine my heart and keep me from thinking I'm right in my own eyes when I am really blind. May I always be accountable to You first, and allow You to be the ultimate Judge in all situations. Instead of blame, help me encourage, lift up, and inspire others. Let me not stumble back into an attitude of blame. Above all, may Your Name be glorified in how I choose to speak, think, and respond as a parent of a teen in crisis.

Amen

BROKENNESS

He heals the brokenhearted and binds up their wounds.
Psalm 147:3 NIV

Of course, it was bound to happen. Fumbling about on a shelf too high for me to comfortably reach, I moved dishes around to retrieve my favorite antique platter. But, my precarious hold on its scalloped edge loosed. I watched helplessly as it slid through my fingers, tumbled to the floor and shattered to pieces. Reduced to sharp shards and broken fragments, my beloved family heirloom lay in ruins, strewn across the kitchen tiles.

I was devastated. Like Humpty Dumpty, I couldn't put my broken dish back together again.

When we think of the word "broken" we often picture something beyond fixing—like Humpty Dumpty and my antique dish. We could try to fix it ourselves with glue. From a distance it may even look flawless—good as new. But, upon closer inspection, hairline cracks at the rupture points disqualify the dish from ever being used for its original purpose again.

This is a fair metaphor for life with a broken teen. And, if we're brutally honest, ourselves. As parents we're brokenhearted over our teen's choices, their illnesses, and their addictions. Because of our inability to fix their wounds, we live with the floodgates of guilt and shame. This is especially tough when we believe it is our duty to protect and love them.

When it seemed my teen and her troubles were slipping through my ability to hold onto with a firm hand, I began to lose my hope and trust in God. The crises in our home seemed too far gone for even God to heal. I sought out other things, outside of God, thinking I could glue us all back together as a family and restore us to my original dreams for us. Before all the brokenness.

But my efforts proved no better than slapping a band-aid over a broken leg. No healing comes of that. I needed to dig deeper for God's answers.

One day I came across a creative art form from Japan called, Kintsugi. It means, "golden joinery." In this process, powdered metals such as gold, join together broken pieces of glass or pottery, bonding them so they can be useful again. This technique fills in hairline-crack flaws, highlighting the very breaking point of the piece to make an artistic statement. A masterpiece! The restored item is not only strong enough to return to its original purpose but shines with a spectacular new beauty.

Pondering on this inspired a change of perspective

in me about broken things. Could my broken family be so restored that we, too, could become an artistic statement masterpiece?

Kintsugi art uses real gold. I found it fascinating to learn that God created us with a trace amount of pure gold in our make-up.* In thinking on this fact, I realized that the God who made us with such a precious material in the mix, is well able to heal us and increase our value therein.

God is the Maker of Masterpieces. The Lord wanted to do more in our lives than just restore our relationships. He planned to use all our painful, fragmented, and shattered moments for His glory, creating in effect, a work of artistic beauty out of our brokenness. He used every crack, chip, and splintered part of our lives, strengthening us with a gold bond, restoring us to our original purposes in Him. In our new, gold-sealed glory, God now uses our family to minister His powerful message of healing broken lives to other families just like us.

How generous and loving God is towards His creation. He heals our wounds and uses our imperfections. Our defects showcase the miraculous power of His renewal in our hearts, mind, body, and spirit.

God is the Great Physician able to heal your deepest wounds. He desires to fill the cracks of your brokenness with gold and make your healing a work of art. Put away your glue and yield your faith towards Him, so He can heal you and your teen, making a Masterpiece for His glory.

Go Deeper

 If you step on a rose and crush it, a sweet perfume rises up with an essence like no other flower. God made you precious like the beautiful rose. There are times when you feel crushed and broken. How can God use you in your brokenness?

 Many who are broken have lost control of their life; feeling that they are beyond repair. Psalm 31:12 says, *"I am forgotten as though I were dead; I have become like broken pottery."* But Jesus is the Divine Healer and delivers those who are broken. Knowing this, how will you allow Jesus to repair your brokenness?

 Our wounds and brokenness are not so big that God cannot heal. Name five ways that God can restore your life, your hope and your spirit?

Meditate on Scripture

My flesh and my heart may fail, but God is the strength of my heart and my portion forever.

Psalm 73:26 NIV

For I am afflicted and needy, And my heart is wounded within me.

Psalm 109:22 NASB

But he was pierced for our transgressions, he was crushed for our iniquities; the punishment that brought us peace was on him, and by his wounds we are healed.

Isaiah 53:5 NIV

Pray

Dear Heavenly Father,

You are the great I AM who knows and sees all things that happen in my life: the good, the bad and the truly ugly. You are the Deliverer and Lifter of my head. Although my flesh and heart may fail, You O God, are the strength of my heart and my portion forever. When I am downcast and wounded, let me take all my burdens, brokenness, and hurts to the foot of the cross. For You were pierced for our transgressions and crushed for our iniquities. Remind me that You were broken for me on the cross and by Your stripes I have been set free from these burdens. May Your glory fill every crack and flaw within. Make me new and restored.

Amen

* The human body is composed of many elements, including gold in trace amounts. According the technical treatise, *The Elements Third Edition*, written by John Emsley and published by the Clarendon Press, Oxford in 1998, the average person's body weighing 70 kilograms would contain a total mass of 0.2 milligrams gold. "How Much Gold is Found in the Human Body," Gold Traders, http://bit.ly/2P2eXDv

"Anything under
God's control
is never out of control."

— Charles R. Swindoll

CONTROL

*Many are the plans in the mind of a man, but it is the
purpose of the LORD that will stand.*
Proverbs 19:21 ESV

As an organizer and leader serving in many positions
through the years, the word "control" has had a powerful
impact in my life. Though, I admit, not always for the right
reasons.

The seed of my control issue took root in my late
teens when I came under the influence of an evil mentor in
the guise of a church leader. This youth pastor/cult
follower, whom I looked up to and respected, abused the
trust I had freely given to him, spiritually, mentally,
physically, and sexually. This left a myriad of open wounds
within me, including the void I felt when, having a baby as
a teenager, I was forced to give my child up for adoption.
Raped, brainwashed, and scarred because of this man's
power and manipulating domination over me, I vowed I
would never, allow anyone to have that much control over
my life again.

So, when my daughter Daniela was in crisis, I wouldn't permit others to help her. I was afraid to trust an authority figure and risk losing control again. I felt I knew what was best for my child and attempted to counsel her myself. I consulted no one. Not even God.

As a parent, I thought my plans and strategies were better than God's. In actuality, they only whipped-up a maelstrom of problems too big for me to handle.

Instead of consulting the Lord as to what I should do to help my daughter in her critical time, I allowed the emotions and pain from my past to dictate how to control the situation. I clung desperately to my rope of control, hanging on with all my might, but to little effect when I watched it slowly unravel before my eyes, and to my horror. When I came to the end of my rope, the gross reality of my helpless condition jolted me to question how much of my control actually helped me. Actually helped my troubled daughter. I needed Godly counsel, and quick!

Meeting faithfully week after week with my own counselor, I began to connect the dots to understand how my need to control had grown out of control. It took months to untangle twenty-five years of anger and confusion knotted-up inside of me. Freed from my need to control and equipped with tools to keep it in check, I moved slowly forward, finally allowing others to help me help my daughter.

I realized that God never intended for us to carry such a weight on our shoulders. Letting go of the pain of an abusive past and the burdensome need to control all aspects of my life by myself, both relieved and released me to tackle my family's issues in new strength.

Have you been carrying this burdensome weight on your shoulders too?

It's never too late to relinquish your need to control to an all-knowing God. He alone is faithful and worthy to be in control over every part of our lives. Even the storms of crisis. When you put your faith and trust in God, He will not abuse it. And when waves of turmoil flood your world, He controls the tide, and will place your life securely on a rock, bringing you to a safe haven in your moment of need.

Go Deeper

 What areas of your teen's crisis have you tried to control? Where did it lead? What is the biggest control issue you have in your life right now?

There are healthy and unhealthy ways to be in control of your teen's life. Name several of each that you are doing now in your life. What do you believe will be the end result for each?

When we release our control to the Lord, He can then step in and start the process of healing our family. What can you do to take the first step of releasing control over to Him?

Meditate on Scripture

Therefore, do not worry about tomorrow, for tomorrow will worry about itself. Each day has enough trouble of its own.

Matthew 6:34 NIV

Do not call to mind the former things, or ponder things of the past. Behold, I will do something new, now it will spring forth; will you not be aware of it? I will even make a roadway in the wilderness, rivers in the desert.

Isaiah 43: 18-19 NIV

For as the heavens are higher than the earth,
So are My ways higher than your ways
And My thoughts than your thoughts.

Isaiah 55:9 NIV

Pray

Dear Heavenly Father,

I know that you are in control of yesterday, today, and tomorrow. Let me look for the new things that You have for me and not ponder on the things of the past. When I feel stuck or don't know what to do, give me direction and a roadway through the wilderness instead of trying to maneuver through on my own. Encourage me to trust You when I don't have the answers, for Your thoughts and ways are higher than mine. When I feel a crisis coming on, remind me to get on my knees to pray. May Your wisdom abound in my life so that my choices are productive and fruit bearing for my family. Help me to release all control to you every day.

Amen

COPING

But he said to me, "My grace is sufficient for you,
for my power is made perfect in weakness."
Therefore I will boast all the more gladly about my
weaknesses, so that Christ's power may rest on me.
That is why, for Christ's sake, I delight in weaknesses, in
insults, in hardships, in persecutions, in difficulties.
For when I am weak, then I am strong.
2 Corinthians 12:9-10 NIV

I casually walked by the kitchen table where a pile of unpaid bills, stacked to the ceiling, lay waiting for my attention. Too bad the checkbook was in the other room-- and just a little too in the red for me to address it anytime soon. I looked the other way and pretended it wasn't there. See, I can cope with bills.

Chronic depression stole my appetite. I can cope with that. I'll just fast and lose a couple of pounds and maybe that will add some persuasive power to my prayer life for my daughter. That'll work. Sure. I can cope with that. Even if it means losing a little more than a couple pounds and a bit a muscle mass. So what if I can feel my organs slide from side to side when I turn over in my bed on sleepless nights.

47

I'm coping because I'm fasting, Right?

My child has issues. I know. I've learned to cope with that. If I ignore it long enough, it'll probably heal itself and just go away. I'll turn down the social invitations, too. I can do this alone. I won't feel so obligated to answer cross examining questions from other parents and people in general. See, coping. It may result in paving the way to loneliness and isolation, to some degree. But I'm okay with that. It's all in the art of coping.

When it comes down to it, you can cope all on your own. Here's my secret best-coping skill I ever mastered: Just. Ignore. Everything. Easy-peasy. Coping.

Most of us instinctively try to solve problems through coping techniques. We research online, read books, watch videos, and depend upon our own limited experience and knowledge to get on the other side of our troubles with a little mental trick or two. Often though, we find that rather than being strengthened in our efforts, we are weakened. When we attempt to deal with our problems on our own, all our coping mechanisms fail because they are merely a fleshly response. trapping us in a cycle of unresolved life issues.

Coping alone fixes nothing. It only limits our ability to overcome. Faith, on the other hand, opens prison doors and sets us free. It pays the bills. It restores the appetite. It redeems relationships.

Our reaction to the constant upheaval in our homes can lead to unhealthy coping methods, such as reaching for an alcoholic drink, a cigarette, or even a prescription painkiller. Some coping methods may be useful, like a weekend retreat or a long overdue nap. But nothing can take the place of the complete rest and peace that comes from a total dependence upon the Lord. In my moments of weakness, had I sought the Lord first, I would not have fallen into the unhealthy coping traps that block the healing God promises us.

Psalm 94:14 says that God never forsakes us. I, on the other hand, often choose to forsake God when I place my trust in my own wisdom. Remember—I'm coping.

When my coping skills didn't work in the times of hardship and difficulty, it was because they were not focused on the Lord. I needed to search for God's power to help me to find new ways of coping that were more than just ineffective band-aids.

Working with a counselor, I learned a lot about making quality coping choices. I practiced new God-given ways to deal with my stress and depression such as journal writing, reading God's Word, and listening to my favorite music for encouragement. I realized that I was not Superwoman and was okay with that. I don't always need to be strong when God is always strong for me. I was coping—in Christ.

With these foundation pieces in place, I said goodbye to my old ways of coping. Growth became evident as I utilized the tools God gave me. The only one who can help us cope with the battles in our lives is Jesus Christ. He endured the cross, so we might be empowered to cope with life in a sinful world through His power.

God's love for you is immense. He delights in giving you a healthy mind, body, and spirit. Don't despair. Stop just coping. The Holy Spirit will uphold you during times of crisis and give you the wisdom to overcome—not just cope. Let us boast in Him for His grace is sufficient in our hour of need.

Go Deeper

 What coping skills have you used in the past to deal with your teen in crisis? Did you find refuge in those skills or with God?

 How is God's power perfected in your weakness during your time of emotional crisis?

 List three ways that you are coping now to get through your turbulent storm. Then list three ways you can cope with God's power as your anchor.

Meditate on Scripture

Trust in him at all times, you people; pour out your hearts to him, for God is our refuge.

Psalm 62:8 NIV

Call to me and I will answer you and tell you great and unsearchable things you do not know.

Jeremiah 33:3 NIV

Come to me, all you who are weary and burdened, and I will give you rest. Take my yoke upon you and learn from me, for I am gentle and humble in heart, and you will find rest for your souls. For my yoke is easy and my burden is light.

Matthew 11:28-30 NIV

Pray

Dear Heavenly Father,

Help me to trust You at all times. Let me pour out my heart to You when I need to find a place to cope for You are my refuge. Please forgive me for not submitting my problems to you in moments of stress and instead using other alternatives to cope. This is not Your will for me. Father, show me how to come to You first with my problems and concerns. Prompt me to guard myself against the attacks of the enemy by adding the full armor of God outlined in Ephesians 6:10-20. Holy Spirit lead me in Word and prayer. Teach me Lord, how to rest in You. For Your yolk is easy and Your burden is light. Impart to me new spiritual tools to cope such as Your Word, and resources to overcome any struggle or crisis that I face, so that You may be honored and glorified this day.

Amen

"The Bible is God's chart for you to steer by, to keep you from the bottom of the sea, and to show you where the harbor is, and how to reach it without running on rocks or bars."

— Henry Ward Beecher

CORRECTION

No discipline seems pleasant at the time, but painful. Later on, however, it produces a harvest of righteousness and peace for those who have been trained by it.
Hebrews 12:11 NIV

"So how would you like me to counsel you?" the pastor asked. "Would you like me to counsel you as a family member, or as a pastor?"

I knew the veiled meaning of those questions. Did we want to be counseled with kid gloves or with a good slap in the face! Daring to be brave, I chose the slap in the face. That day, I got slapped. A lot.

I'd arrived at the counseling session expecting to be reprimanded. I felt three feet smaller than my adult self, justly weighed down by correction and discipline. Caught in my sin, like a child snagged stealing cookies from the cookie jar.

Let's be honest, no discipline is joyful. Correction, gentle or otherwise, can be mortifying and painful to endure. As parents, my husband and I made some huge blunders, too humiliating to mention. Guilt fell heavily upon us, often pelting us like a hailstorm, leaving dents and bruising in its wake. We sometimes had a tendency to get defensive. But our excuses and sojourn in the land of denial had to stop. As husband and wife, we accepted our error in judgment and sin. Only then could healing begin.

What sins and mistakes are we talking about?

- Not making decisions together as parents in unity
- Letting set boundaries slide
- Giving into our daughter's demands
- Opening our home to people who should not have been there—who were part of the problem
- Jeopardizing the welfare of our daughter by not applying consistent discipline
- Permitting manipulation with no correction
- Following our parent guidelines instead of God's

And this was just the tip of the iceberg.

With our hearts laid bare before our pastor in counseling, we came to understand our desperate need to change, or suffer further dire consequences, enabling our daughter in future crises.

Parents strive to be great caretakers of their children. They raise them to be the best, instruct them in the way they should go, and one day, hope to hear the words, "You did good Mom and Dad." But sometimes along the way they may get sidetracked, swept off course in navigating their children through turbulent waters.

How can we make sure we are following God's lead and not falter in our parenting over and over again?

God's written Word is a map designed to lead us through often treacherous seas with Christ at the helm. We are moved, like the rudder of a ship by the Holy Spirit steering. When we allow ourselves to be so directed, we are saved from veering off course, in need of correction.

We will hit tips of icebergs. We will make blunders. We will fail. We will sin. We will need course corrections. Just like we correct and guide our children, God will do the same for us if we humble ourselves and allow Him to. We can move forward towards forgiveness and repent of our sin as we continue in faith with our Heavenly Father.

I would rather accept God's loving correction than to have regret, sorrow, and a lifetime of heartache. Discipline is hard. But the rewards are plentiful: peace in your home, a teen on the road to healing, and parents who have learned valuable lessons along the way.

Go Deeper

 God corrects us because He loves us. Explain how you would be willing to listen and act upon that correction to improve your family's life?

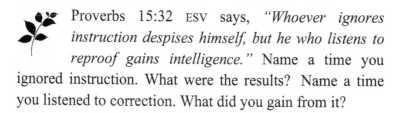 Proverbs 15:32 ESV says, *"Whoever ignores instruction despises himself, but he who listens to reproof gains intelligence."* Name a time you ignored instruction. What were the results? Name a time you listened to correction. What did you gain from it?

 Correction and discipline go hand in hand as it trains us to become spiritually mature and humble.

If someone were to correct you today in an area where you know there is an issue, how will you choose to respond?

Meditate on Scripture

Blessed is the one whom God corrects; so do not despise the discipline of the Almighty.

Job 5:17 NIV

If you reject discipline, you only harm yourself; but if you listen to correction, you grow in understanding.

Proverbs 15:32 NLT

All Scripture is God-breathed and is useful for teaching, rebuking, correcting and training in righteousness.

2 Timothy 3:16 NIV

Pray

Dear Heavenly Father,

Your loving reproof and correction reveals how much You care for me and my family. I know that Your discipline is good for me, keeping me from acting foolish. Instill in me humility to receive your instruction with joy. As I watch for your correction, grow me in understanding. Being disciplined can be painful, but in the end, I know it will bear a harvest of righteousness and peace. This also produces a stronger foundation for parenting. Keep my spirit in check. Show me when my motives are wrong. May Your Word bring teaching, training, and righteousness in our family's lives.

Amen

DECEPTION

Teach me your way, O LORD, that I may walk in your truth;
unite my heart to fear your name.
Psalm 86:11 ESV

For a long time, I deceived myself thinking Daniela would outgrow her problems as she matured. When others brought to my attention some of her deceptive patterns, I ignored them. I justified her actions and told them they didn't understand.

Blinded by deception, I could not see our situation from any other perspective. Due to my distorted grasp of our family's true condition, my teen's healing took longer because I blocked opportunities for real help.

Coming to the end of my denial and ignorance, I asked God to expose the truth. Desperate for answers to our teen's problems, God revealed to me how I had succumbed to deception.

First, He alerted me to comments made by others such as, "Your child is manipulating you." Then, I noticed little behaviors from my daughter I'd not observed before including words and actions that I repeatedly overlooked or denied their existence.

I did not believe myself to be a bad parent because I turned a blind eye. Many parents of troubled teens are genuine, loving parents struggling with misguided and prideful responses to their child's disturbing behaviors.

Our compassion for our child becomes an obstacle keeping us from the truth. We often go over and above appropriate measures to accommodate their needs, even when it is not in their best interest. This is especially true when either the child—or others—call our choices into question, accelerating the crisis to a whole new level.

Christ loves us fully. His love is complete with discipline, correction, and calls to obedience rooted in truth. This love teaches us to stay close to His truth and fend off the lies of deception. When I strayed, following deception and denial, God's love pursued me to draw closer to Him and thereby see truth.

Little by little, God used life situations and His Word to convict me and bring the light of truth to my understanding. He spoke to my heart through friends I respected and those in spiritual authority. But the biggest wakeup call came when God allowed calamity to fall upon us—seeing Daniela in her worst crisis.

Daniela wanted to be loved so much that she often allowed herself to be a victim. This was especially true in regard to a relationship with a boyfriend who, unbeknownst to us, involved himself with the Blood Gang. They call it "Blood" for a reason. The more Daniela feared abandonment and the loss of him in her life, the more she put herself in danger, as well as her family.

She overheard many things regarding the gang and their activities, but because she struggled with memory issues, she did not retain the details of these secrets. Even so, she heard enough to know that if she exposed any information outside of her boyfriend relationship, someone would get hurt.

In an attempt to protect herself, she kept up a charade that everything was fine, hiding the true nature of her situation. But I have learned that things hidden, eventually rise to the surface.

In due time, her behavior became more erratic. She would cry, then rage in anger, then tremble, overwhelmed in fear. I questioned her over and over concerning this and always received the same answers, attributing her behavior to her anxiety, mood disorders, or depression. I fell for her excuses every time because I loved and trusted her.

This all changed when she was arrested, and I found myself in the police station with her. The events capsized her life, as well as ours, like a rowboat overturned on choppy, storm-tossed waters.

Deception knocked me off the course the Lord required me to walk as a responsible parent—a hard reality-pill to swallow. I believed lies, judging something to be not so bad, which allowed it room in my daughter's life. This interfered with God's role to heal my teen.

The biggest lesson I learned: Truth is deceptive when it is your truth, not God's truth.

Don't rely on your truth. Seek God's truth. The only way to steer clear of deception is to focus on biblical truth through God's Word.

Go Deeper

 Some synonyms for deceived are duped, fooled, gulled, tricked, defrauded, entrapped, and ensnared. Have you recognized areas in your life where these words might apply? How can you incorporate truth into your life so that you will not be deceived again?

 Now that truth is exposed. How can you defend and protect yourself from being misguided by the world and your own thoughts?

Ask yourself: Did *my* truth mislead me away from the real truth of Jesus Christ? Write one or more incidents where this has happened to you.

Meditate on Scripture

Guide me in your truth and teach me, for you are God my Savior, and my hope is in you all day long.

Psalm 25:5 NIV

Do not conform to the pattern of this world but be transformed by the renewing of your mind. Then you will be able to test and approve what God's will is—his good, pleasing and perfect will.

Romans 12:2 NIV

Let no one deceive himself. If anyone among you thinks that he is wise in this age, let him become a fool that he may become wise.

I Corinthians 3:18 ESV

Pray

Dear Heavenly Father,

Thank you that I can put my hope in You all day. It is easy to conform to the pattern of this world and deceive ourselves into believing and approving lies. Guide me into Your truth—your wisdom—instead of relying on my own. Unite my heart to fear Your name, Lord. Transform and renew my mind as I draw close to You. Teach me Your ways. Holy Spirit, open my eyes to see truth so I will not believe in a lie again. May I seek out a righteous fear and hunger for truth and not be deceived. Give me discernment to see clearly so I do not fall back into deception.

Amen

"God allows us to experience the low points of life in order to teach us lessons that we could learn in no other way."

— C.S. Lewis

DEFEAT

Give your burdens to the LORD, and he will take care of you. He will not permit the godly to slip and fall.
Psalm 55:22 NLT

Pop! Pop! Pop! Soaring balloons of a promise for help burst in defeat, plunging to the ground in pieces.

Finding a therapist or an excellent program specializing in troubled teens can be tedious, mind-boggling, and expensive. A review of available options exhausts the spirit and deflates hope with the painstaking demands of information overload. I might come upon a gold mine and get excited, analyzing everything about them. Then click a link revealing the fees and insurance policies. My heart sinks wondering how many more I'll have to weed through before discovering a workable solution.

I lost count on the number of phone calls made to counseling offices. My voice sounded like a broken record: *"Do you accept this insurance? What is your sliding scale as a cash patient? Do you accept this insurance? What is your sliding scale as a cash patient? Do you accept this insurance? What is your sliding scale as a cash patient?"*

Each defeating answer to my questions planted a seed of hopelessness. About eighty-five percent of my carefully researched options did not take our insurance. To find the fifteen percent which did compared to finding a one-inch treasure box on a twenty-foot-long ocean mural. The proverbial needle in a haystack.

Frustrated in defeat, I searched online one more time for counseling resources. Lighthouse Solutions popped up on the screen. They featured a free hotline to match clients with health providers in my area and cater to my budget, insurance, and more. Through this resource, my daughter found the right counselor—and so did I.

Even so, matters deteriorated when bills required payment. My husband, a barber, ran a business swiftly growing extinct in most places. Dwindling cash flow didn't allow me to address the bills flooding my mailbox. Depression took over when Hope left the building. As a mom and caretaker for my troubled teen, going back to work to make ends meet became a must, not a choice.

Then the Lord reminded me of His comforting Word in Psalm 55:22, calling me to give all my burdens to Him with his promise to take care of me. I had been carrying a heavy load of multiple burdens myself, never truly allowing God to take them from me. He convicted me to stop this pattern of doing things alone, apart from Him. I made the choice to let God carry my backpack of troubles. This lightened my load, allowing me to rise from defeat and walk again.

God invited me to give my burdens to Him and trust that He will take care of me and not allow me to slip or fall. Just when I thought God didn't hear or care about my setbacks or complications, He made a way forward. Everything fell into place in my understanding when, driving home one day, I passed a church sign stating: "Can God? God can!"

My Faith lifted like a balloon soaring high, rising up in His promises. When Faith lifts the veil of Depression, Defeat flees.

God turned the tide of our fortunes. We watched how He smoothed the path so we could arrive at every appointment on time with every fee paid. A new job brought provision both financially and with workable hours. This allowed me to be available for my teen at home, in addition to making all our counseling appointments.

I stand amazed at God's faithfulness. He knew our financial status. He knew we were disheartened and beaten down. He understood the difficulty and embarrassment of not making enough money to pay our growing bills. My God, who owns the cattle on a thousand hills, also knew our needs. The funds were there when we needed it.

You see, we may have felt defeated, but God defeated so much more through Jesus' death on the cross and resurrection to new life. Like those balloons of promise rising up, we are risen in Him and His provision in all things necessary to our lives. I believe God will not let us be conquered in what looks like lost hope.

My favorite verse on faith when I feel defeat coming says, *"If you don't stand firm in your faith, you will not stand at all."* Isaiah 7:9 NIV Defeat is not a condition God wants us to live in. We must redirect our mind and spirit regarding our faith in Him.

The more you place your faith in Him and His promises, the more He will move in your life and family. Victory begins there.

Go Deeper

Deuteronomy 20:1-4 and John 16:33 tell us how to obtain victory. Read these scriptures and write down what actions you must take to rise above defeat.

As a servant of Christ, we are never truly defeated unless we allow the enemy to make us feel defeated. Are you willing to release those feelings of defeat so that He can replace them with victory?

C.S. Lewis, a defiant atheist for many years, relentlessly pursued answers to his questions about God until he found God. As a parent, will you relentlessly pursue the healing of your family no matter the crisis or obstacles? What can you do to keep from being defeated in your pursuit?

Meditate on Scripture

I have told you these things, so that in me you may have peace. In this world you will have trouble. But take heart! I have overcome the world.

John 16:33 NIV

Be joyful in hope, patient in affliction, faithful in prayer.

Romans 12:12 NIV

Now to him who is able to do immeasurably more than all we ask or imagine, according to his power that is at work within us.

Ephesians 3:20 NIV

Pray

Dear Heavenly Father,

Please forgive me for Defeat to capture me when I give up too easily because I lack trust in You. Give me the strength to fight against the enemy's lie that our situation is beyond hope. Remind me that in You we have peace because You have overcome the world. Remove the thoughts that persuade my mind to think it is not worth it. Exchange them with thoughts of hope, patience during affliction, and faithfulness in prayer. Reveal to me how to overcome and be thankful at all times even when I don't see an answer right away, for I know that You can do immeasurably more than all I can ask or imagine. When victory comes, may I be an example to our teen that there is no such thing as Defeat when God is in charge.

Amen

"I am fallen, flawed
and imperfect.
Yet drenched in the grace
and mercy that is found
in Jesus Christ,
there is strength."

— Adam Young

DENIAL

*If we say that we have no sin, we are deceiving ourselves
and the truth is not in us. If we confess our sins,
He is faithful and righteous to forgive us our sins
and to cleanse us from all unrighteousness.*
I John 1:8-9 NASB

Have you ever been confronted with a situation too
unbelievable for you to accept as truth? I certainly did not
want to believe my teen would self-harm, physically hurt
someone, or hack a computer. But she did.

A parent does not want to believe that their child
has become an alcoholic or addict. A parent does not want
to believe that their child steals, has an eating disorder, or is
promiscuous.

In fact, our teens are troubled with many serious
issues. We must raise our children with eyes wide open,
face the storms head on—believe and inwardly accept the
truth.

When we are confronted with the raging turbulence
of our teen's trouble, our brains jump to denial mode for
mental and emotional survival. We look away from the

reality of our situation and say it is not possible, or pretend it is not there. A common reaction for many parents.

I know it was for me.

Denial is dangerous. It affects the future of the health and welfare of our teen in a serious way. This type of denial, fully grown to infection, festers within a parent's heart and mind becoming sin in us. As parents, God has called us to be accountable for His gift to us: our children. To purposely turn a blind eye to their hurt, or not provide tough love to keep them from trouble, is both reckless and dangerous.

I know this sin all too well. In the past, I often let things slide. Decisions I made in the heat of denial almost cost my daughter's life. This sin is an affront to our holy God and saddens His heart. We must confess it, repent, and stop living in denial.

Some symptoms of denial that can put you and your teen in the red danger zone are:

- Lying, or giving half-truths to others, when we purposely refuse to accept the truth of our teen's crisis.
- Deceiving others with long drawn out excuses for our child's behavior.
- Unwillingness to get help for the one in crisis through our denial that a problem exists.
- Putting self above the one who is hurting when our wants become more important than their needs.

- Enabling them by giving reinforcement of destructive behaviors that worsens their illness or addiction.

God desires to restore families in broken places. But if we choose to deny there are fractures in our family, in our teen's mental and emotional health and development, how can He help? If we continue in the sin of denial, our child will remain in crisis mode.

Once we admit the truth, believe and accept that there is something very wrong, the next step is to confess the sin of denial. Repent and stop denial in its destructive tracks. This is the only way we can partner with God and start the restoration process.

Need help? Reach out to a friend, your pastor, or counselor. God is faithful to all who humble themselves, die to self, ask for forgiveness, and walk in His truth.

Go Deeper

According to Webster's Dictionary, the word denial means a "refusal to recognize or acknowledge; a disowning or disavowal." Matthew 26:75 records when one of Jesus' closest friends and a disciple, Peter, denied that he knew Christ not once but three times in on the night He was condemned to die on the cross. Peter was fearful to be associated with Jesus in light of such a horrific situation. As a parent, what truth have you denied about your teen's crisis that you would rather put a distance between you and it? Is there a crisis in your life that you have denied?

 When we are in denial of our teen's issues, what are some ramifications of that denial? For them? For you?

 Christ did not deny us on the cross when He knew we were broken inside, full of sin, and imperfect in every way. He did not make claims to His own innocence and throw us under the bus, left to find our own way of salvation from our sin. How can you use that example of selfless, unconditional love to change your own situation?

Meditate on Scripture

Then he said to them all: "Whoever wants to be my disciple must deny themselves and take up their cross daily and follow me."

Luke 9:23 NIV

So I say, walk by the Spirit, and you will not gratify the desires of the flesh.

Galatians 5:16 NIV

But if anyone does not provide for his own, and especially for those of his household, he has denied the faith and is worse than an unbeliever.

1 Timothy 5:8 NASB

Pray

Dear Heavenly Father,

Thank you, Lord, that You never deny me as Your child. I have hindered my relationship with You by walking in sin. Lord Jesus, I acknowledge and repent of my willful and sinful ways. Help me deny myself and take up Your cross daily as I walk with You. When a crisis occurs, let me be led by the Spirit so that I do not give in to the desires of the flesh and return to denying the truth. There have been times when I have not provided for my family and have denied my faith to believe You are powerful to heal my hurting family. Lord, forgive me. Let me, instead, call out Your Name in my time of need. I choose to seek Your Godly wisdom and counsel. If there is pride in my heart, break it down and pull it out. Plant seeds of humility so that You will be honored. I praise You for reigning over our family today.

Amen

"Relying on God has to start
all over everyday,
as if nothing has yet
been done."

— C. S. Lewis

DEPRESSION

So do not fear, for I am with you; do not be dismayed, for I am your God. I will strengthen you and help you; I will uphold you with my righteous right hand.
Isaiah 41:10 NIV

The war against Daniela's issues cut through our lives like a deep gorge with no bottom. Crisis after crisis pressed in, engulfing us in countless lost battles. Darkness and despair pervaded every aspect of my life. Stressed, exhausted, and mentally zapped, I stopped fighting for my daughter's rescue.

> *What I feared has come upon me; what I dreaded has happened to me. I have no peace, no quietness; I have no rest, but only turmoil.*
>
> Job 3:25-26 NIV

At one point, I just gave up as a parent, a wife, and friend. My weight loss brought me to a mere ninety-five pounds. My husband, concerned for my welfare, struggled in knowing how to fix what was happening and felt as helpless as I did.

I forget to eat my food. In my distress I groan aloud and am reduced to skin and bones.

Psalm 102:5 NIV

I started to believe that I might follow in the depressed and suicidal footsteps of my daughter. As time slowly wore on, God became just a random thought. My emotions numb. My prayers absent. Despite my fear, I just didn't care anymore. I felt paralyzed.

In the second year of a deep depression, I received a very vivid dream. I saw myself on the threshold of a dark abyss. I wasn't the only one there. Daniela stood nearby, in more danger than I, for she had accepted the abyss as her final resting place.

This dream, powerful and realistic, shook me to the depths of my spiritual core and became the catalyst to seeking help for our family. My eyes opened wide seeing the dark side of Daniela's severe depression and suicidal tendencies. In the following days, she was diagnosed with PTSD, chronic depression, and a mood disorder among a list of other things.

If we look at the biblical record, others suffered from depression too. Job, David, and Jeremiah were a few who struggled, in addition to many prophets in both the Old Testament and New Testament. There were no medications available to manage their depression. Counselors and psychiatrists were unavailable for therapy sessions.

Instead, they cried aloud to the Lord from the depths of their hearts. They laid themselves bare before God, raw and vulnerable.

Today, we have friends, family, and professionals in the counseling field to support us when the waves of turmoil pull us under, drowning in our despair. God did not mean for us to live alone in this way.

In Exodus 17:10-13, Moses, with his arms raised to the heavens to keep the Amalek warriors from advancing against Joshua and people of Israel, grew fatigued from physical exhaustion. Noticing this, his close aids, Aaron and Hur, immediately stepped in and braced each arm up. As a result, Joshua and his troops crushed the enemy.

The Aarons and Hurs in my life were my counselor, spouse, and a close, trusted friend. In time, I grew to see how God's Word provided guidance for me to know what to do in troubling situations. I also found strength in worship music, where certain songs supported me with encouragement. For the first time, I felt armed and prepared to unload that bundle of woes and move on towards recovery and healing.

Parents of troubled teens need the vital assistance of an Aaron and Hur in their painful journey. We must seek out and receive the commission of others to share in our struggles. When we do, the Lord does not waste time in advancing His plan for us in the battle.

Depression is real. It affects a lot of parents who have teens in crisis. Don't wait until you feel like your life is unbearable. Don't be fearful of what others think. The Lord is with you and will help you. He will be your life-jacket to keep you from drowning. Trust in His guidance. He will carry you to the safe places where you will be upheld by His Spirit, and the Aarons and Hurs he sends for support.

Go Deeper

Believers in both the Old and New Testaments—and throughout church history—have dealt with depression even though they had a strong faith in God. Although medications and therapeutic resources may not have been available to them, how did they ask God for help and how did God respond?

Many parents who deal with a teen in crisis fall into the trap of depression. What are some safeguards you can take to give you power as you climb out of darkness?

NOTE: If you struggle with depression, I highly encourage you to seek counseling for it ASAP. Depression can be due to stress over a teen in crisis or a sign of a more serious issue such as a medical or mental illness/disorder. Don't wait. Call someone today. As an added resource, there is a parent test for depression in the Appendix at the back of this book.

Meditate on Scripture

The cords of death entangled me, the anguish of the grave came over me; I was overcome by distress and sorrow. Then I called on the name of the LORD: "LORD, save me!"

Psalm 116:3-4 NIV

He lifted me out of the slimy pit, out of the mud and mire; he set my feet on a rock and gave me a firm place to stand. He put a new song in my mouth, a hymn of praise to our God. Many will see and fear the LORD and put their trust in him.

Psalm 40:2-3 NIV

Why, my soul, are you downcast? Why so disturbed within me? Put your hope in God, for I will yet praise him, my Savior and my God.

Psalm 42:11 NIV

Pray

Dear Heavenly Father,

Thank you for being at my side and giving me courage to keep going on. Though I felt like the cords of death had entangled me and distress and sorrow surrounded me, You saved me Lord when I called on You. You lifted me up out of the slimy pit of depression. When I was downcast, You gave me hope. You set my feet on the solid rock and a firm place. Give me a new song in my mouth and a hymn of praise to You. Renew my spirit from the dry and weary place and let it overflow with Your goodness. Lord Jesus, I know You will continue to show me how to discern the course of action I need to take to be in a healthier place. If and when those struggles come, send me an Aaron and Hur to hold back the walls of depression until You touch me with healing and win the battle.

Amen

DESPAIR

Why are you in despair, O my soul?
And why have you become disturbed within me?
Hope in God, for I shall again praise Him,
for the help of His presence.
Psalm 42:5 NASB

Imagine yourself as a fly on the wall. You could easily spot a parent with a teen in crisis. One may have tears flowing down her cheeks. Others are hunched over with their hands holding their heads in anguish—words barely audible from their mouths. Some are numb. They sit and stare as if they are in the Twilight Zone. Some cut the conversation short when asked about their kids.

I have been this fly on the wall. Observing. I have been this parent, too.

The gut-wrenching turmoil of watching your teen spiral out of control leaves you empty and hopeless. You observe the slow destruction of their life through risky behaviors and lifestyles. Trying to prevent the dire outcomes of such choices on your own without professional support or resources leaves you depleted and defeated.

Maybe you're the parent of a teen who struggles with confusion over their sexual identity. Maybe their eating disorders have put their health in jeopardy. Maybe their mental illness has driven them to the edge of insanity. You could be the parent of a son or daughter who has overdosed on drugs. Or possibly, you are a parent of a teen who can't stop self-harming. Whatever it may be, the result produces constant distress in the parent with no discernable light at the end of the tunnel.

Our fears build mountains of despair—insurmountable with no relief, no one to aid us, and no way out. We panic, wandering lost and, at times, inconsolable.

How in the world can we overcome this level of despair? Can God see the pain we feel? Can He understand our uncertainty wondering if there is any rescue for our troubled teen? Will we ever see the miracle we so desperately need? Deliverance from our despair?

In my days of despair, I often wondered if Daniela would succeed in taking her life. I felt helpless. Day and night, I poured out my heart to God hoping He might hear me—sometimes unsure if He even cared to. I cried to the Lord, "Please reach Daniela in ways I cannot before it is too late!"

My despair and agony brought me to my knees and my face to the floor. I implored God to intervene. I asked the Lord to halt every evil plan and scheme the enemy had to destroy my daughter. I would at times, not give up until I could feel God's presence to let it go.

I did not receive a clear-cut answer—no big revelation or vision of how God would move in her life. But what I did know, without a doubt, is that God's faithfulness in all things is unchanging.

Dear Parent—God's love for your child is greater than your own. How can you not trust and put your hope in Him now, knowing He is always at work on your behalf? On behalf of your child? His child?

The opposite of despair is hope. In our eyes, everything looks impossible. In Matthew 19:26 NIV Jesus said, *"With man this is impossible, but with God all things are possible."*

We serve a God who created the universe and every living thing in it. He knew us, our sons, and daughters before we were born. God sees the beginning and the end of all things and knows every detail of their life.

He knows every detail of your life, too.

There are many mothers who know their children live harmful and damaging lifestyles. Months turn into years, yet these mothers never stop seeking God daily to protect their children and bring their prodigals back home. It is difficult to keep going. Some are tempted to give up because of constant pain and hurt without a pinhole of light that change is on the way. Fortunately, their love for God endures and they know in their hearts that He is the only answer. They press forward and ask God to carry them through until the end.

That end is the new beginning of a child's life as we hear the stories from a parent's son or daughter who share how God rescued them. Yes, even from the brink of death they are rescued, all because a faithful parent prayed through their own despair. These parents took their emotional response and offered it to our Heavenly Father who saves and is faithful to bring our wayward ones back into His fold. What a great reward for these parents to see the fruit of their prayers fully revealed in due season.

> *I would have despaired unless I had believed that I would see the goodness of the LORD, in the land of the living. Wait for the LORD; be strong and let your heart take courage; yes, wait for the LORD.*
> Psalm 27:13-14 NIV

Go Deeper

 When all seems like there is no answer, how can you turn your eyes to the Lord and change despair into hope?

 What does God ask of us when we are in despair?

Proverbs 15:3 reminds us that God's eyes are always watchful. He is not just looking out for your son or daughter's welfare but yours as well. In what other ways is He watching over you and your family?

Meditate on Scripture

Let us hold unswervingly to the hope we profess, for he who promised is faithful.

Hebrews 10:23 NIV

Therefore, do not throw away your confidence, which has a great reward. For you have need of endurance, so that when you have done the will of God, you may receive what was promised.

Hebrews 10:35-36 NASB

When I said, "My foot is slipping," Your unfailing love, Lord, supported me. When anxiety was great within me, Your consolation brought me joy.

Psalm 94:18-19 NIV

Pray

Dear Heavenly Father,

You are always near to understand and respond to my despair and in times of trouble. Center my thoughts on Your promises of hope to get through each day. Remind me to not look at my situation with eyes of impossibility that would throw away my confidence. Instead, build my endurance to the many possibilities that You have promised in Your Word as my reward. Encourage me to praise You at all times. Calm my anxious heart. Let me prayerfully seek You during my moments of anguish and fear so that help will come quickly in my time of trouble. For Your consolation will bring me great joy.

Amen

DEVASTATION

*If only my anguish could be weighed
and all my misery be placed on the scales!*
Job 6:2 NIV

When I discovered a secret Daniela had hidden from me for some time, my heart sank like a torpedoed ship drowned in the sea of devastation.

My daughter had recently risen above one of the most difficult times in her life. However, her emotional state remained unstable and I feared that her next few choices could set her back. I reached out to a mentor, a psychologist, and a special counselor, but their words only fell on Daniela's deaf ears. Fearful anxiety flooded my heart at the direction her latest poor choice might take her.

I prayed. I prayed hard. I begged for God to change the course Daniela had set her eyes upon. I reasoned that if God had come through at other times in Daniela's life, why not this time, too.

Despite all those prayers, words of advice, and counsel, the answer that I hoped for didn't materialize. No words could describe the deep sense of devastation I felt. Speechless. There was nothing else I could do but cry and ask God, "Where are You?" Daniela had improved by leaps and bounds with the promise of healing. But now, my hopes and dreams for her future receded like the waves rolling onto the beach, then out again into the churning depths of darkness.

How much more could I possibly take? My co-workers, Ruth and Debbie, who knew the Lord, saw the devastation in my expression, creased across my face, as I walked through the door at work. They didn't need to know the details. "We'll pray!" is all they said—and got down to holy business. I knew I was in good hands.

For weeks, these dear friends supported and prayed for our family. They offered to add some of my duties onto their own workload to lighten my burden more. These women, who struggled in their own troubles, put aside their needs to uphold me in mine. I didn't have to drown in my sorrow alone.

While my tears continued due to all the wreckage surrounding my family, God was already moving in my daughter's life. As the months wore on, she appeared to develop a maturity unseen in the past. She began to discern how her choices, birthed from a swirl of weakened, lonely, turbulent emotions, were unwise. Accepting ownership of her waste and ruin, she recognized the devastation in her life which caused her to ask important questions. She realized that her refusal to see what God wanted and not asking for His wisdom produced costly mistakes. A true wake-up call.

God birthed something new in her life as well as mine. Healing took hold and the dark clouds covering our devastated, desolated fields, lifted. "Thy will be done" became my battle cry, unseating "my will be done." Praying in this way, Heaven's doors opened wide. God saved my crushed spirit. He can save yours, too.

Go Deeper

 Devastation comes in various forms. It envelopes you with a sense of complete ruin, destruction, and desolation. In what ways have you've been devastated by your teen's choices?

Luke 15:11-32 shares the story of the prodigal son, whose father was devastated at his son's choices through rebellion and sin. This father may have even felt rejected as well as humiliated. Despite the sadness that he carried due to his son's choices, he still embodied compassion and forgiveness towards his wayward child. How can you relate to this father and prodigal son?

Do you believe that God can work through your child despite how devastated you feel? How then can you pray for your child?

Meditate on Scripture

I cried out to God for help; I cried out to God to hear me. When I was in distress, I sought the Lord; at night I stretched out untiring hands, and I would not be comforted.

Psalm 77:1-2 NIV

The LORD is close to the brokenhearted and saves those who are crushed in spirit.

Psalm 34:18 NIV

Do not let your hearts be troubled. You believe in God; believe also in Me.

John 14:1 NIV

Pray

Dear Heavenly Father,

My battered heart is in pain. My hopes are overpowered and defeated. I cried out to You for help and to hear my distress. Oh, how I seek You with outstretched arms. You, O Lord, are close to my broken heart. As I look to You, may I not be troubled any longer. I know all things— including all my crises—are seen by You and do not pass through my life without Your knowledge or permission. I will trust in You, for the seen and unseen as we navigate on rough seas. You are the repairer and restorer of all who have been devastated. Thank You for Your healing power and never-ending love for me and my family.

Amen

DISAPPOINTMENT

*"My thoughts are nothing like your thoughts," says the
LORD. "And my ways are far beyond anything you could
imagine. For just as the heavens are higher than the earth,
so my ways are higher than your ways and my thoughts
higher than your thoughts."*
Isaiah 55:8-9 NLT

Did the insurance company decide to no longer pay for
your teen's visits to the counselor? Did the program your
child entered not be as effective as you hoped and
expected? Did your teen have a set back into their addiction
or illness? Did your son or daughter promise to do better
only to fail miserably?

If you've answered "Yes!" to any of these questions,
then you have experienced disappointment. We have such
high hopes, dreams, goals, and desires for our children's
future. When those expectations are not met, we are often
disappointed in the outcome.

We can also become disappointed in ourselves. Did
well-intentioned attempts to help our teen produce wrong
choices on our part? Through spoken words, did we show
our teen how much they were valued, loved, and cared for

or only devolve into harsh lecturing? I'm sure your list of disappointments in them are just as long as their disappointments in you.

Many of us have seen God turn impossible situations around for His glory. Does He turn around disappointments too? The answer to that is a resounding "YES!"

In our journey working with counselors, we found one with whom we bonded well until she became ill. So ill, in fact, that her recovery would take a year or more. She announced her decision to not continue her practice which greatly impacted our family.

As disappointed as we were to hear this news, God met our need and opened the doors to someone new and just as good. We felt God's peace instantly as we transitioned with our new counselor. Even better, she guided us into areas which we had not yet explored.

By trusting God when disappointment comes, He may choose to lead us in a new way that we may not like, or a place unexpected. He created our child; therefore, He knows exactly what is best for them. My mother once said, "God's answers may not be easy or what we like, but He always does provide."

If you get too focused on disappointments, you may miss God's plans and blessings in front of you. Listening to God's voice is the only advice you should consider. When you allow Him to take charge, you will never be disappointed. Remember, a temporary disappointment to us is an opportunity for God to work wonders beyond our imagining.

Go Deeper

 Name people in the Bible who experienced disappointment. How did God reverse their disappointment by bringing them to a better place?

 How will you submit your feelings of disappointment to God, and in obedience, submit to His ultimate purposes fulfilled?

 Our disappointments are God's opportunities. What does that mean in your life?

Meditate on Scripture

Your kingdom come, your will be done, on earth as it is in heaven.

Matthew 6:10 NIV

Sustain me, my God, according to your promise, and I will live; do not let my hopes be dashed.

Psalm 119:116 NIV

"For I know the plans I have for you," declares the LORD, "plans to prosper you and not to harm you, plans to give you hope and a future."

Jeremiah 29:11 NIV

Pray

Dear Heavenly Father,

Lord, I feel so disheartened at times by disappointment in my children and even disappointment in myself. Father, help me to submit my ways to You, for Your ways and Your thoughts are perfect. I know that all things work together for good of those who love You and are called according to Your purposes. Help me not to hang on to disappointments but see them as opportunities for You to step in and minister Your more perfect will. Yes Lord, let Your will be done on earth as it is in Heaven. Sustain me Lord, according to Your promises. For You have a great plan for me and my family. Plans to prosper us and to give us a future and a hope.

Amen

DISCOURAGEMENT

May the God of hope fill you with all joy and peace in
believing, so that by the power of the Holy Spirit
you may abound in hope.
Romans 15:13 ESV

Have you ever endured a marathon of discouragement? My hopes and expectations for Daniela would ride high like a surfing wave when she turned a corner in getting her life back on course. Sadly, it didn't last long. A riptide of discouragement would rush in with a wipe out.

My child didn't purposely plan to dash those hopes, but her life was a never-ending cycle of one wave after the other. I never knew if I could ride the wave or be pulled under. It was to the point that encouragement was not in my vocabulary or attitude.

I lost count as to how many times I had been blindsided. I wanted to give up. I wanted to crawl under a rock and hide. I didn't want to think about how many more crises it would take to push me over the edge where I would literally lose it.

There were moments when I wallowed in downright depression. I barely functioned. I hate to admit it, but suicide crossed my mind more than once. Gone were the days of feeling positive that things would eventually work out. Where was hope when I needed it?

Discouragement happens. It's part of life. When you have a teen in crisis, it shows up like a rhythm of waves in the water; continuous and relentless. So where do you even begin to combat discouragement when it rears its ugly head, especially when you have had more than what most parents deal with?

Believe it or not, disarming discouragement starts with an attitude adjustment. This won't be easy, and you need God's help. These four steps go a long way to remaining encouraged when clouds of discouragement loom on the horizon:

1. Grieve the things that you had hoped for in your child. Then let them go. This takes time—it's a process.

2. Release your expectations of your teen to God and let Him worry about them. After all, He loves your teen more than you can think or imagine.

3. Move forward with being positive. Commit to getting healthy and do the things you enjoy. Make it a priority to see your friends and get Godly counsel for yourself.

4. Thank God for the many blessings you have, including the gift of your teen.

When I did these four things, I let go of lingering discouragement in my life. From that point, God's words became larger and more powerful in my life. Reading the Word of God aloud built up my faith and optimism. Within the passages of Scripture, I personalized it for me. This made such a difference. By doing so, His truth is proclaimed and fights off the thoughts of discouragement and schemes of Satan.

I continued to bolster encouragement in my life by turning up the volume on my Praise and Worship music while singing along. When you praise God in worship, you allow the Spirit of God to move through you with Divine inspiration. This is one way the Holy Spirit can powerfully jump-start hope in your life.

Place Scriptures that minister to you around your home. This is a great reminder that God's peace and presence is within reach when you long for it. God is very aware of every aspect of your child's life. There is nothing that He can't handle when it comes to your teen. God is there to shepherd you. Seek Him in all things and you won't be disappointed.

Go Deeper

 Discouragement is another word for defeat. How can we change this heart attitude and permit God to cultivate hope instead?

What has been the biggest discouragement that you have faced? In Joshua 1:9, God commands us, *"do not be discouraged."* How can you apply this to what you are facing?

God sees your situation now and the future. In Jeremiah 29:11 He promises to give you hope. How does that alter the way in which you view discouragement now?

Meditate on Scripture

What then shall we say to these things? If God is for us, who can be against us?

Romans 8:31 ESV

Trust in the LORD with all your heart and lean not on your own understanding; in all your ways submit to him, and he will make your paths straight.

Proverbs 3:5-6 NIV

Have I not commanded you? Be strong and courageous. Do not be afraid; do not be discouraged, for the LORD your God will be with you wherever you go.

Joshua 1:9 NIV

Pray

Dear Heavenly Father,

You have not given me a spirit of fear or discouragement but one of hope and joy. You are for us! Who can be against us? I know, Lord, that there will be times I need to wait and hear from You. Teach me to not lean on my own understanding on how to do things, but to submit to you so you can show me the true way. Although discouragement comes in this world, You give courage and hope just at the right time because You have overcome the world. As I wait, fill me up with stamina and durability to persevere. Let peace overflow in the times of uncertainty so that it overrides any moment of anxiety. Help me to trust You at all times and to always praise You. It is through my praise that You extend grace for whatever I am facing. Thank You, Lord.

Amen

"We need never shout
across the spaces
to an absent God.
He is nearer than our own
soul, closer than our most
secret thoughts."

— A.W. Tozer

DOUBT

But let him ask in faith, with no doubting,
for the one who doubts is like a wave
of the sea that is driven and tossed by the wind.
James 1:6 NLT

One day, I shout with overflowing exuberance in my voice, "I am going to have complete faith and trust in my God for the deliverance and healing of my daughter!"

The next day. Ugh! Not so much. I'm too drained to pray. When is she ever going to get healed? *Probably never,* I answer myself in my own wisdom.

Isn't it easy to doubt God's faithfulness when your prayers don't get answered in the time you have allotted for an answer? For me, it appears as if all my prayers fell silent in God's ears while the problems in our home with Daniela increased.

Why couldn't I have faith like a child? Children will believe anything. If you ask a child if they can fly to the moon, they will say yes and then tell you how. Oh, how I desired to have childlike faith to believe God would deliver and heal our broken home.

So why and when did my faith become fettered with so much uncertainty? As always, a battle rages within our flesh every day, beating us down mentally, physically, and emotionally. We are attacked on every side down to the deepest fiber of our being. This results in the voice of Doubt proclaiming that God can't hear us when we call for help or ask Him to rescue our teen from their destructive behaviors.

When pondering this dilemma, I begin to understand the tug of war between Faith and Doubt that the prophet Elijah encountered in I Kings 18. God told Elijah to challenge King Ahab, his wife Jezebel, and the prophets of Baal and Asherah—all 800 of them. In this quest, whoever was able to get their god to bring down fire from heaven, served the True and Living God. When the prophets of King Ahab tried, they failed. No fire from the heavens for Baal's company or their sacrifice. But, through obedience and faith, Elijah called upon God and consuming fires from Heaven fell upon his sacrifice, making a mockery of Ahab, Jezebel, Baal, and all the false prophets.

Queen Jezebel was angry. She decided to kill Elijah because of the shame and embarrassment she sustained in her defeat. Elijah's initial thought was not that God's would protect him. Instead, he chose to run for his life, fearful of Jezebel on the warpath. Wearied from running, his faith diminished, and doubt set in. Exhaustion made Elijah, vulnerable to discouragement and doubt. He didn't call on God to rescue him out of his dangerous dilemma. Instead, he just ran away to hide.

God eventually confronted him, but not with rebuke. Instead, God refreshed him and encouraged him. God knew Elijah was tired and discouraged. He also knows that you are, too.

So, what do we do when we feel like our life has wavered more towards doubt than faith? Remind ourselves that we are not alone. God is with us just like He was with Elijah—no false prophets necessary. God doesn't want us to run away from Him when we begin to doubt, but to run towards Him. That is how faith is built-up in our hearts, minds, and strength. In the midst of our crisis when we have no other way to turn, look up. We can always turn upwards towards Him, leaving our doubts far behind as we are lifted-up.

Call upon Him to refresh you. Ask God to bring others in your life to raise you up in faith and hope.

Going Deeper

 We know it is easy to fall into discouragement and imagine doubt. What three ways can we turn our doubt into faith?

 There are great men of faith in the Bible whose faith was tested through their trials. When they failed, they revealed their doubt in God. Thomas, a disciple and close friend of Jesus, doubted the risen Lord in John 20:26-28. How did God respond to Thomas in his time of doubting?

Name others in the Bible who also struggled with doubt. How did they overcome it?

Meditate on Scripture

He replied, "Because you have so little faith. Truly I tell you, if you have faith as small as a mustard seed, you can say to this mountain, 'Move from here to there,' and it will move. Nothing will be impossible for you."

Matthew 17:20 NIV

If you do not stand firm in your faith, you will not stand at all.

Isaiah 7:9 NIV

I rise before dawn and cry for help; I have put my hope in your word.

Psalm 119:147 NIV

Pray

Dear Heavenly Father,

Forgive me for doubting your faithfulness to me. It reveals unbelief and distrust in my heart. Guide me to spiritually grow my faith by ordering my steps and correcting my attitude. Quicken my mustard-seed-faith to stand strong, able to move mountains in Your name. Nothing is impossible with You. May my faith not be tossed like the waves of the sea, pulled under by problems in our family. When my faith crumbles, leaning towards doubt, lift me up, strengthen and activate my spirit to trust in You.

Amen

ENABLEMENT

Take no part in the unfruitful works of darkness,
but instead expose them.
Ephesians 5:11 ESV

Your toddler asks for a cookie out of the cookie jar. You have told him no multiple times already and reprimanded him before sending him on his way. After all, it's almost dinner time and no desserts before dinner. Within minutes, he returns to try one more time to get his favorite cookie. Tired of hearing him, you cave-in to the cookie request. Unknowingly, you have just set in motion the pattern of enablement.

Now, this little toddler is a full-grown teen and he isn't looking for cookies. In place of a cookie, it is money, punishment reduction, begging to get the car keys, or hanging out with friends known to be bad news. As you respond to your teen, part of you wavers. You want your relationship with your teen to stay intact, but at the same time, you must remain the parent in authority.

The complication is that our emotions get in the way of correct parenting. This happened quite often in my own household. I set the rules and had a long talk with my children. Somehow though, each time I gave way to my daughter's wishes and wants which were opposite of the rules set. Later, I'd ask myself, *What just happened? She didn't throw a tantrum. She didn't plead till I surrendered. Why did I capitulate to her demands?*

In fact, she used some very convincing tools common for the training of enablers: tears, her depression, her suicidal threats, her cutting, and her abandonment and rejection stories. In the end, it was her manipulative ways and my weakness that became the pinpoint of many problems.

This is not the type of help our teens need. Our continued modeling of enabling behavior eventually caused nightmares as well as danger in her life. I know from experience that being an enabling parent produces more darkness in the home, not light. It buries the truth and, in our case, wasn't exposed until it was almost too late.

In Exodus 32, the Hebrews complained that they wanted things their way. Apparently, God's plan wasn't quite what they had hoped for. God gave them everything they needed for their redemption from slavery and journey to the Promised Land, including a pillar of smoke by day and pillar of fire by night to guide them as they wandered through the desert. For the people of Israel however, this was not enough.

While Moses spoke with God on Mt. Sinai, Aaron confronted an impatient people tired of waiting for Moses to return with the Lord's direction. Aaron could have stood resolute in what he knew was right and dealt out a bit of tough love to correct the people saying, "NO!" to their mutinous desires. But, instead of dispensing discipline to God's people, Aaron gave in to their demands and threats to worship an idol in place of the one true God. Aaron knew to worship idols was sinful, yet he crumbled under the pressure to please the people.

Does this sound familiar? Do we, too, crumble under the pressure to please our teen?

Showcasing their sin and rebellion, the Israelites continued to worship idols. They would pay a hefty price for their sin—death. I am sure Aaron never forgot the weight of his decision to let the people walk in such disobedience.

When we fall into the trap of enabling our teens, the ramifications cannot be altered. We will unfortunately have to live with any and all consequences earned by not following God's Word in parenting our children. If we truly love our children, we will make every effort to not give in to their negative behaviors.

God gives us wisdom to guide our children in the right direction to produce healing and life. It will be hard at times. We may feel as if we have squashed their freedom by making them angry or hateful towards us. However, their response to our leading in God's way is their choice— not our responsibility. When disobedience is allowed, it causes greater pain for our teen or young adult—as well as ourselves—than were they to obey contrary to their misguided desires.

Today, be strong! Don't be an enabler. Give in to God's plan and guidance, not your teen's. He will show you what you need to do and give you the power to do it.

Go Deeper

 Name a time in which you enabled your teen? What was the outcome of this enabling?

 If your teen were to come to you now and put you in a position in which you can correct with God's wisdom or enable to keep things quiet in your home, how will you respond?

 What is the difference between helping and enabling a person?

Meditate on Scriptures

However, if you do not obey the LORD your God and do not carefully follow all his commands and decrees, I am giving you today, all these curses will come on you and overtake you.

Deuteronomy 28:15 NIV

What shall we say, then? Shall we go on sinning so that grace may increase? By no means! We are those who have died to sin; how can we live in it any longer?

Romans 6:1-2 NIV

If any of you lacks wisdom, you should ask God, who gives generously to all without finding fault, and it will be given to you.

James 1:5 NIV

Pray

Dear Heavenly Father,

I have sinned before You by giving in to enabling behavior. Forgive me Lord for not heeding Your wisdom and Your Word. Please give me the courage and power to stop this pattern that only encourages darkness and not light. Make me accountable to You Lord for my actions. I know that when I do not obey Your commands and decrees set in Your Word, curses follow and overtake me. Show me how to apply discipline that will benefit my teen and our family. Give me the tools to help me stand firm in the right decisions that are honoring and pleasing to You. When I feel like I am weak and ready to fall back into enabling thoughts, show me immediately the consequences of this sin. Encourage me as I walk this path of better choices and obedience, seeking Your wisdom in all things—including how to respond when I am confronted with enabling behavior.

Amen

"Is prayer
your steering wheel
or your spare tire?"

— Corrie Ten Boom

ENVY

A heart at peace gives life to the body,
but envy rots the bones.
Proverbs 14:30 NIV

Did you ever wish you could be *that* family? Have you ever been jealous or envious as you watched other families laugh, bond, and enjoy each other's company?

I've often been envious of those who seemed to have perfect families with no problems. Even if they had unseen problems, I never felt our family made the grade. It became the norm to compare ourselves with other families around us, to have the false belief that no family could be more broken than ours.

Our family was far from perfect. We struggled with a depressed teen who had severe abandonment and rejection issues. While her peers talked about fun sleepovers and parties, our daughter talked about how much she hated others and wanted to bring harm to them and herself. She wished for death all the time. In her mind, if she was unhappy, why should others be happy.

Every day I questioned God in my heart: *Why do we have to go through this life of constant struggle and never-*

ending pain? Why do we live in despair while other families seemingly don't?

This was so unfair. And to be honest, it sometimes felt like a punishment.

The truth is, God understands our pain. He always knew Daniela's issues, and our crises. He knows everything. Nothing escapes Him.

Looking back, I could see how fixated I had become on what I did not have: a normal happy family. As a result, I was blind to God's plans and purposes or the gifts that God gave us in our daughters.

Being envious eats you alive. Once it sets in, it devours down to the very bone. After a while, I started to feel less of me and more of E.N.V.Y. I didn't need this. I didn't want this. I had to find a way to unload this burden of jealousy at the foot of the cross.

In opening my heart and mind to healing at the cross, I immediately thought of all the joy-filled details surrounding the adoption of our children. Sometimes we have to revisit the initial moments of our greatest joys to guard our hearts against the nasty twins of Envy and Jealousy. This was a great place to start.

The Lord arranged for us to adopt both of our daughters from Eastern Europe. As unwanted orphans in their country, their lives would have been destined for the sex trade industry or they'd have been married off at the age of twelve. I thank God for the adoption of our precious daughters. I can't and won't have to imagine a life with that kind of horrific future for them.

From a spiritual perspective, chances are my daughters would not have come to know God. I am so thankful today that they have a knowledge and acceptance of Christ as their personal Savior. Their future was in His hands from inception—which included being a part of our family. God confirmed His sovereign and beautiful plan, through His Word.

> *Do not be afraid, for I am with you; I will bring your children from the east and gather you from the west.*
>
> Isaiah 43:5 NIV

As soon as I understood the magnitude of what God did for us, those feelings of envy turned into feelings of gratitude, contentment, and peace.

Right now, revisit the memories of how your child was placed in your arms. Doesn't it feel good to think that God brought your child to you as part of His awesome plan? In light of this truth, re-examine your heart and move those envious thoughts towards a godly repentance. We cannot allow such feelings to linger one extra minute.

But how can we keep moments of jealousy from rearing its ugly head? A good example to help deter from envy is the story of Joseph and his brothers.

In Genesis 37, we read the stormy saga of Joseph's life. His brothers did not like how their father favored Joseph and put him on a pedestal above every other. Like an angry, brewing cyclone, their hatred ruled their decision making, and left them with unregulated emotions. Contemplating his murder, they opted to sell him into slavery, instead. This choice resulted in years of family separation, and later, years of famine in the desert where their bones might have rotted.

But God's grace redeemed both their envy and Joseph's life when what they purposed for evil was turned to good. Through a series of events, Joseph rose to governor of all Egypt, second only to Pharaoh. He administrated the food stores for all the land and people during seven years of famine. Fortunately, God's plan to deliver Joseph's brothers and family under his leadership brought them to repentance and reunification. Laying down their envy by owning their sin, they came to be filled with gratitude for their brother, contentment in their situation, and peace that the Lord was taking care of them in their dire need.

God frees us from sin at the cross—including those who lay thoughts of jealousy and envy at His feet. In place of these feelings, He restores hope through gratitude, contentment, and a heart full of peace—despite what our eyes may see in our family circumstances. In due time, our spirit fills with life and envy is a distant emotion of the past.

Go Deeper

 As a Christian, have you ever viewed others or things with envy within the family of God?

 List some ways to surrender thoughts of envy, leaving them at the Lord's throne.

 In Galatians 5:1, Paul says not to be subject to a yoke of slavery. If we are not careful, we will be a slave to jealousy. How can we find release from the slavery of envy if we are entangled in it?

Meditate on Scriptures

It is for freedom that Christ has set us free. Stand firm, then, and do not let yourselves be burdened again by a yoke of slavery.

Galatians 5:1 NIV

But the fruit of the Spirit is love, joy, peace, forbearance, kindness, goodness, faithfulness, gentleness and self-control. Against such things there is no law. Those who belong to Christ Jesus have crucified the flesh with its passions and desires. Since we live by the Spirit, let us keep in step with the Spirit. Let us not become conceited, provoking and envying each other.

Galatians 5:22-26 NIV

Pray

Dear Heavenly Father,

I subject myself to Your authority and ask that You destroy the roots of envy in my heart. For I know that in Christ, I have been given freedom and have been set free from this destructive yoke that binds me. Guide me and help me walk in Your Spirit. By submitting to Your obedience, I can then bear the Fruit of the Spirit as recorded in Galatians 5:22-23: love, joy, peace, patience, kindness, goodness, faithfulness, gentleness, and self-control. Living fruitfully like this, I cannot be controlled by envy again. Show me how to keep my eyes fixed on you and to bless others the way you have blessed me. I know You have in store for me a powerful testimony of love and healing.

Amen

EXPECTATIONS

My soul, wait thou only upon God;
for my expectation is from him.
Psalm 62:5 KJV

You left the counseling session with high hopes for your teen. You're all smiles and ready for the new change. Before you know it, a new development transpires soon after you get home and your happy train derails.

Maybe you're at work and receive a phone call that your son was just arrested. Drug paraphernalia was found on him after he left the rehab. You shake your head in disgust. You wonder how this could be when you thought he had already hit bottom.

You find your daughter in the bedroom crying uncontrollably. She went into a meltdown and you thought she was doing so much better. Your fears have now risen to a new level. Your gut aches. You really believed she had made tremendous improvement.

Do any of these situations sound familiar? I've lost count on how many times my expectations were dashed within a month, a week, a day, and even a split second. We shouldn't be surprised but somehow, we are still left stung in unexpected shock.

I've heard my daughter say, "I don't feel a need to cut now" or "I don't want to die anymore." I got excited as hope rose within, as if those words were now written in cement. No sooner had I heard this, that the situation took a dramatic turn and I found my expectations sinking faster than a submarine hit with a mine in the depths of the ocean.

Is it wrong to have expectations? No. The important thing to master is where to place those expectations. This adds more pressure--a set-up for disaster--when goals are not met. Our great advancements suffer as back to the starting line we go.

Heartbreak is hard to deal with. When expectations consistently fall short, we begin to lose faith and patience. This happens in both our hopes for our teen and in our own lives, as well. The problem lies in the fact that we place our expectations on the wrong foundation of what we think is progress--an unsteady, stormy sea. We need to put all our expectation on Jesus, the Rock on which we stand. So stationed, there is no fear of Him failing.

God never changes. He is the same yesterday, today, and tomorrow. He has our best interests at heart, including our children.

For this reason alone, we need to put our eyes on God and expect Him to do what we are not able to. This is also true as we deal with the boisterous, up and down surging waves of our teen's journey. Our only requirement is to keep our eyes on Him, the Author and Finisher of our faith.

God is faithful, giving us hope when ours is diminished. So, let your expectations be built on nothing less than Jesus Christ. You will be amazed at the outcome.

Go Deeper

 Name all the times God has been faithful to you when your expectations failed.

 Name three ways you can put your hope and expectations in Christ?

 Why is it important to wait on God for your expectations?

Meditate on Scriptures

And my God will supply every need of yours according to his riches in glory in Christ Jesus.

Philippians 4:19 ESV

There is surely a future hope for you, and your hope will not be cut off.

Proverbs 23:18 NIV

The LORD upholds all who fall and lifts up all who are bowed down.

Psalm 145:14 NIV

Pray

Dear Heavenly Father,

May my soul wait upon you O God. Focus my eyes on Your expectations and not on my own. Teach me to trust in You to supply my every need in every expectation according to Your riches in glory. May I not overwhelm my teen or myself with goals too high to obtain. When we fail, make mistakes, or go through tough times, reveal to us that Your grace is truly sufficient. When my expectations falter, remind me that You uphold all who fall and lift all who are bowed down. From this moment forward, I will put my expectations in Your hands. You are my hope yesterday, today, and forever, and I will not be cut off.

Amen

FAÇADES

*If we claim to have fellowship with him and yet walk
in the darkness, we lie and do not live out the truth.*
I John 1:6 NIV

Caring for a teen in crisis is hard work. Even more so when
you try to keep it a secret. You create a façade to hide
behind and hope that no one will see the truth. You depend
on this smokescreen to survive the turbulent ride on the
choppy waves of a broken family. This façade becomes
your perception of truth in everyday life to family, friends,
and even God.

A façade is an illusion—the idea of seeing
something different than reality. It's comparable to a city
street on a movie set. They're all just fake fronts. Façades.
In essence, façades deceive the understanding and distract
from the truth. You may be thinking, *That sounds like
lying. I don't lie.* But consider: Aren't there times when
little excuses you may use—perhaps little white lies—help
you deceive others, diverting them from the truth of dark
family secrets, including that of a hurting family?

I wanted my heart to be in the right place and keep
my teen protected from those around her. I did not want

others to snoop around in an attempt to decipher her issues. I didn't believe it was any of their business. But, hiding the truth caused off-the-chart stress levels in my life. Would Daniela go over the edge if she learned of something I said or did—out of love and care—in my effort to protect her? There were times I thought she would.

Looking back, I did not trust those who did have our best interests at heart. Instead, I feared truth being exposed. I assured myself that our situation was not horrific and would ultimately get better in time. I lied to myself and hid behind my façade.

When we create façades, we build a wall between us and our Heavenly Father, whose very nature is truth. We choose to blindfold ourselves, led by the enemy's lies.

I lived in a world of self-erected façades. In doing so, I demonstrated a lack of faith in place of living with God's truth no matter what. His truth would have given me a life of freedom. But my choices only led to a life of bondage.

Truth is powerful enough to break any chain, stronghold, or evil scheme that may befall our families. When we question God on why our prayers aren't answered, it could be because we have lived or believed a false-front illusion. A lie. Cowering behind a facade.

Tear down the façade and come into the light of freedom and restoration. Fear no longer has a hold on your family when truth is exposed. Trust in Him instead of false perceptions. You'll be thankful for truth as it sets you free.

Go Deeper

 Where in your life have you built a façade to hide a truth?

 What is the worst that can happen if your façade is exposed? What is the best scenario?

 God's Word is a beacon of truth for us to follow so that we don't sink into the waters of living behind a façade. Trust in Him. You can be released from shame and guilt that has taken root within. List 5 steps you can take to lead you out from behind the façade you may have built.

Meditate on Scripture

Therefore each of you must put off falsehood and speak truthfully to your neighbor, for we are all members of one body.

Ephesians 4:25 NIV

Do not lie to each other, since you have taken off your old self with its practices and have put on the new self, which is being renewed in knowledge in the image of its Creator.

Colossians 3:9-10 NIV

From Your precepts I get understanding; Therefore I hate every false way.

Psalm 119:104 NAS

Pray

Dear Heavenly Father,

I have lived behind my façade for long enough. Lord, break down the barriers I've erected so that truth can come to the light. Release me from carrying this burden of pretending things are okay. May I cast off the lies and schemes of the enemy and speak truthfully to those around me, for we are all members of one body. Show me how to put on the new self through You, so that I can be renewed in the knowledge and image of my Creator. Thank you, Lord, for You have revealed truth and opened my eyes. I am now set free from the spirit of illusion and the lies of Satan. May my life from this point on be guided by Your truth, which gives me understanding and keeps me from falsehood.

Amen

FAILURE

And we know that for those who love God all things work together for good, for those who are called according to his purpose.
Romans 8:28 ESV

I'm a fixer. Always have been, always will be.

Unfortunately, I couldn't fix the biggest problem I had in my life—my troubled teen. A parent is supposed to fix things. We fix boo-boo's, colds, and fevers. We fix the broken, precious items our kids love: stuffed animals with an eye chewed off by the dog, bicycles with a wonky chain, phones run amuck, games with missing pieces, and toys lost, then found, right under the little one's nose.

How was I able to repair all those things and not be able to heal Daniela's pain? I tried herbal medicines, therapies, and searches on the internet. None of it worked. I begged, cried, and pleaded with Daniela to stop her destructive behavior.

Yes, she was sorry, and told me so. Then she went out and repeated her destructive behavior all over again.

Looking back, the failures on my part as a parent were clearly evident. Overwhelmed with an acute sense of my failures, I couldn't pull myself together enough to ask for help. I was afraid of judgment. Of hearing those horrid words, *"You failed."*

Instead of reaching out for help for my child, I enabled my child. I was so worried about her self-harm, her suicidal ideology, and many other issues, I felt sorry for her and tried to comfort her. This did not change anything in her life. What it did do was allow her to use me, like a doormat for her to walk on. Being so close to the critical situation my vision blurred the truth of the matter, distorting each detail along the way.

I wasn't the only one affected by failure. My husband felt like he failed because he didn't discipline more. We were all so worried about Daniela falling apart that he didn't put his foot down as a father and set boundaries. We allowed Daniela's friends to come into our home when we really should have said no from the very beginning. When she received her driver's license, her rebellion and patterns of destructive behavior escalated. She took advantage of our weakness and we all paid a hefty price for it.

Most importantly, we neglected to teach her about the Father's love and desire to heal her. In fact, we relied on our own self-help for healing which worsened her multiple issues.

We realized we were in way over our heads trying to help our daughter in our own strength when faced with the ultimate consequences of our actions. In essence, the storm currents pulled us under water, drowning in our problems and crises.

When we reached that point of despair, we frantically pushed our hands up through the waters crying out to God, "I can't do it anymore Lord! Take over!"

God's response was swift and merciful: "It's about time." That's all He wanted to hear from us.

Despite my wrong choices and tormenting thoughts of personal failure, God used those significant moments in my life to draw me closer to Him. In time, failures help us realize that a perfect parent is not reality. But, in His mercy, God redeems each and every one of our failures, transforming them into teachable moments graced with love, and forgiveness.

God allowed me to see that it's okay to not be able to fix things. Especially people. That's His job, not mine. When I owned this truth, the heavy burden I carried in needing to fix my daughter lifted from my shoulders. I could stand once again.

In such a victory, failing along our way isn't a bad thing. My imperfections showcase God's perfection. If I can learn through my failures, then I can accept them with more dignity when they do come.

Remember, everything works together for His good and for His purposes. He will give you the wisdom and guidance you need so your problems will no longer be fraught with failure but renewed with rejoicing.

Going Deeper

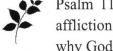 Proverbs 24:16 NASB says, *"For a righteous man may fall seven times and rise again."* (See full verse below.) What does this Scripture teach regarding failure?

 Psalm 119:77 says that it is good for us to have affliction. Look up this full Scripture and write out why God allows affliction in our lives.

The worst thing we can do is to repeatedly recall past failures in our mind. What does Philippians 3:13 say about this?

Meditate on Scripture

Humble yourselves before the Lord, and he will lift you up.
James 4:10 NIV

For the righteous falls seven times and rises again, but the wicked stumble in times of calamity.
Proverbs 24:16

And I am sure of this, that he who began a good work in you will bring it to completion at the day of Jesus Christ.
Philippians 1:6

Pray

Dear Heavenly Father,

I have often failed as a parent. Some of those failures were based on my own selfish thinking to believe I could fix everything. I now know that I am not able to do so. I need You, Lord, to fix me first. By not leaning on You or seeking Your Word for advice and counsel, I open the door for failure. I am so thankful Lord, for how you took my failures and turned them around for Your good and for Your purposes. Yes, even if I fall seven times, You will help me get back up seven times. Redirect my focus for victory and impart to me the wisdom I need to grow and learn, so I can guide my teen in the proper way.

Amen

"I'm not afraid of the devil.
He can't handle the One
whom I'm joined to."

— A.W. Tozer

FEAR

*For God gave us a spirit not of fear
but of power and love and self-control.*
2 Timothy 1:7 ESV

Quietly, discreetly, I gathered every cutting instrument in the house. Who would have thought I would need to sneak about and tip-toe in pitch darkness to collect scissors, pins, tweezers, and knives, then carefully hide them in the deepest corner of my closet.

Daniela had not detected how often I surveyed her body for new cuts. Much like a detective, I was determined to look for clues of the next self-injury. Would it be more severe than the last time? A constant vision of driving furiously to the hospital to save her life tortured my mind.

I could never leave her alone. This meant watching her all hours of the day. At night, my fear intensified. With little sleep, I peeked into her room to make sure she was safe. I noted every pattern of self-harm as well as highs and lows of her mental state. Some days I could relax. Other days the fear of losing her in this way gripped me like a fishing net with sinkers threatening to pull me under the waves.

Who could I turn to for help? I feared that, if others knew, their perception of me would change. They would be disappointed in my ability to mother my children. I feared being shamed. I feared that I would be called a horrible parent. I was even fearful of letting God have control.

I took matters into my own hands, allowing fear to steer my life into the open stormy seas. In uncharted territory, I realized this type of mindset had to stop.

Fear is a choice. We can allow fear into our life, or we can resist it and stand in the power of God. I got tired of living in fear. When I chose to utilize God's power and let Him take control, the situation changed. The day came when I bravely revealed my daughter's cutting addiction to a select group of people whom I thought I could trust. The seas that had opposed me calmed enough for me to get my bearings. The grip of fear, retreated.

Consider the biblical account of David and Goliath. Did David fear his opposition?

Young shepherd, David, stood before a colossal Goliath, the biggest man among the Philistines. David could have been overpowered by inexperience and fear if he believed he was alone. But David loved and trusted God. He knew he didn't need to fear because God's power was greater than any foe he would ever face.

The Philistines and Israelites watched his every move, convinced of David's defeat within seconds. David, however, knew he was not alone and didn't walk before Goliath in fear. He walked in God's power. Rising above fear, he took hold of his sling and slung the first and only stone needed to knock Goliath down. His bold faith enabled him to conquer Goliath.

When we walk about in fear, we are saying to God, "I don't have enough faith in You to see me through."

As one dear friend said to me once, "I am more afraid of the pain this situation will cause, than I am willing to trust God in it." In such a place, we forget that our God is larger than our circumstances—and our teen's issues. We don't need to walk in fear. God asks us to trust Him and His power will be supplied to us in His perfect time.

How do you operate in faith and abandon fear? Romans 10:17 NKJV says that *"faith comes by hearing, and hearing by the word of God."* When we read and apply the Scriptures to the issues we face, faith incubates and stirs in our heart. The Word is a seed and our heart is the soil. We know the fruit of faith has blossomed when, in times of crisis, we can speak the Word of God to our troubles. Thus, fear is dispelled, and the living Word of God is made manifest in our situation.

This type of faith moves mountains. The impossible becomes possible (Mark 9:23). So, the question we need to ask ourselves is this: Are we bearing the seed of faith or fear when we speak?

Going Deeper

 What type of faith or fear do you encounter when your teen goes through crisis?

 Fear can cripple your spiritual life. What can you do to turn those fears around and make your life foundation solid, securely based on faith in Christ?

 Write down five fears that you are dealing with now, and five ways God's Word tells us He can deliver you from those fears.

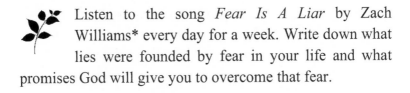 Listen to the song *Fear Is A Liar* by Zach Williams* every day for a week. Write down what lies were founded by fear in your life and what promises God will give you to overcome that fear.

*https://youtu.be/1srs1YoTVzs

Meditate on Scripture

I sought the LORD, and he answered me; he delivered me from all my fears.

Psalm 34:4 NIV

The LORD is my light and my salvation—whom shall I fear? The LORD is the stronghold The LORD is my light and my salvation—whom shall I fear? The LORD is the stronghold of my life—of whom shall I be afraid?

Psalm 27:1 NIV

When I am afraid, I put my trust in you.

Psalm 56:3 NIV

Pray

Dear Heavenly Father,

Give me peace to overcome fear which so easily plagues me. May I feel Your everlasting presence around me wherever I go. I know You have not given me a spirit of fear but of power and love as well as a sound mind (2 Timothy 1:7). You have commanded me to be strong and courageous. Because You are my Light and my Salvation, I need not be afraid or discouraged. Encourage me to put my faith in You when fear confronts me. Answer my cries of distress and deliver me from all of my fears as I call out to You. Let me not be dismayed by the things I see. Lord I pray that you will uphold me with Your righteous right hand. May faith rise above fear as I travel this road of parenting my teen in crisis.

Amen

"Endurance is not just
the ability to bear
a hard thing,
but to turn it into glory."

— William Barclay

FRUSTRATION

I will instruct you and teach you in the way you should go;
I will counsel you with my eye upon you.
Psalm 32:8 ESV

By my sixth attempt to find a competent counselor for Daniela, the word "frustration" barely described my state of mind. The list of fails might be laughable if they weren't so frustrating:

- **Number One** counseled via one-word answers on a chalkboard. Needless to say, he quit counseling not long after to find a new career.
- **Number Two** couldn't provide enough time in their schedule to see us.
- **Number Three** accused our teen of acting as a cancer patient because she wore a wig to give her confidence. As you probably could guess, it was the last time we laid eyes on her.
- **Number Four** was forced to say goodbye to us in order to recover from a serious illness.
- **Number Five** did not have enough experience, in my humble opinion, to deal with Daniela's deep issues.

Frustration.

Exhausted, overwhelmed, depressed, and sinking into a ocean of hopelessness, I feared my daughter's problems would worsen if she did not receive good Godly counsel. I agonized. I prayed. I looked for God to intercede in our situation. Right. Now.

Often, loving our teen means wading through the waters of frustration. Fixes do not come easily. When we think we have survived the crash from one wave, another crash startles us with surprise, knocks us over, and leaves us gasping for air. In those moments, we want to just give up on everything.

God sees when we are drowning at the end of our faith that keeps us afloat. He swoops in as our life preserver and places us on a firm foundation again. We are encouraged, lifted above our frustrations so our hope is not depleted. God's goodness cannot be surpassed.

Though the answers to our prayers delay and we battle frustration, God sees beyond the need to answer our prayers on our timetable. As the months passed while looking for the right counselor, we realized God was working things to give us the desires of our hearts and witnessed much growth in Daniela's life despite the setbacks.

As her mother, I experienced Christ's love for me through every disappointing detail of the process. I may have kicked, screamed, and yelled out in frustration, but God's mercies were new for me every morning. And, in due season, even though I doubted it would ever happen, God answered my prayer, providing a counselor Daniela both respected and loved. A perfect fit in His perfect time.

Many of God's people in the Bible experienced frustration. Moses was frustrated with the disobedience of the people of Israel wandering in the desert. Joshua was frustrated at the lack of faith in those who doubted they would ever possess the Promised Land. Jeremiah the prophet was heartbroken, frustrated because of those who refused to listen to God's words.

But consider: What if they had not walked through those frustrations? Would they have grown in perseverance, faith, and trust?

Our trials are often the means by which we mature in the Lord. Our family wandered for a long time through a frustrating trial in search of the best counselor for our teen. But God was with us every step of the way, available in His capacity as our Wonderful Counselor (Isaiah 9:6). He is never too far from our trials or frustrations.

Hand over your frustrations to the Lord and let God take control. Allow God to teach you and show you the way to go in such times. His eyes are always upon us. Make sure your eyes are always upon Him.

Go Deeper

 Write down a time you were frustrated. How did God show you that He is able to deliver you from your frustration?

 Frustration often leads to bad attitudes and negative behaviors. How can you keep these things at bay and not fall into pitfalls of sin when you feel frustrated?

 God wants us to cast all our cares upon Him and to be thankful in all circumstances. How can doing these two things change your circumstances or outlook within your situation?

*Note: The key to good counseling is dependent upon the fact that your teen and family want it. The best counselor is Jesus Christ. He is the only one that can give good counsel and sound wisdom. Seek a three-fold cord of wise advice through the Word of God, pastoral guidance, and those trained in the mental health and medical field.

Meditate on Scripture

In their hearts, humans plan their course, but the LORD establishes their steps.

Proverbs 16:9 NIV

The LORD makes firm the steps of the one who delights in him.

Psalm 37:23 NIV

Consider it all joy, my brethren, when you encounter various trials, knowing that the testing of your faith produces endurance.

James 1:2-3 NASB

Pray

Dear Heavenly Father,

Help me to cast all my frustrations and cares at Your feet. When I am overwhelmed, let me look up towards You and not down at the situations that frustrate me. When I try to set a course, establish my steps so my choices will not lead me into frustration. Teach me to be thankful at all times, even when it is hard to see the positive side. Keep me from developing a wrong attitude in trying times. Give me discernment so I know the direction You are calling me to walk in. Give me wisdom in my future decisions and confidence to always know that all things work together for good for those who love You and are called for Your purposes.

Amen

"The gospel declares that
no matter how dutiful
or prayerful we are,
we can't save ourselves.
What Jesus did
was sufficient."

— Brennan Manning

GUILT

Therefore, there is now no condemnation
for those who are in Christ Jesus . . .
Romans 8:1 NIV

Accusatory voices resounded in my head: *This is your fault.*
You should have listened to God. Look at all of the stupid
mistakes you made. You enabled your child to be this way.

If I had a penny for every time I condemned myself
over the actions of my child, I would be rich. My penny jar
is empty, but my guilt jar has often overflowed as a result
of all the bad parental decisions I've made in my life.

As a parent, I felt the need to be perfect, to have no
flaws, or leave any room for mistakes. I wanted to be
responsible and accountable for my children. But real life
intervened and failure took root in our home life. For years
my guilt piled up like loads of dirty laundry, reeking to the
point of where I risked passing out. I could barely look at
myself in the mirror. When I did, guilt condemned me. I
didn't know how to peel off the layers of guilt that I wore
like a mud mask.

A close friend reminded me that even the best parents in the world cannot control what their children do. They have free will and a sinful nature. True. Parents make unwise choices and so do children. However, it troubled me I could not separate my personal guilt from the destructive choices my children made.

.

There is a fine line between accepting our mistakes and our sin, verses being bombarded with condemnation from Satan. Just one look at your teen or young adult in crisis and you can't help but wear the guilt label as a parent. You evaluate every motive and action regarding your child to see what wrong turn you may have taken.

Satan, the Father of condemning guilt and lies, loves to remind us of those wrongs. From the moment I woke up in the morning, Satan's words throbbed, pounding through my head all day and into the night with reverberating accusations: *It's your fault your kid doesn't want anything to do with God. You're the one who didn't do enough as a parent. You pushed her into rebellion. You made her worse, not better.*

Days on end this continued. I couldn't look into the eyes of other parents, or even in my own mirror, knowing everything that was going on within my broken home. Satan appeared to be winning. Judging myself by Satan's standards, my gavel hammered out: *Guilty!*

How much longer was I going to live this way? I was tired of it. I wanted out.

The day arrived when I reached a breaking point, tired of living under the burden of guilt. I stopped and confronted my enemy, *Enough with the guilt!* I refused to allow Satan to emotionally abuse me anymore. *No Satan! You can no longer judge and condemn me as a parent. I am redeemed and set free through the blood of Jesus. I have been forgiven, am under His authority, and no longer under bondage.*

If we do not remind ourselves—and Satan—of what Christ has done for us on the cross in defeating the power of the enemy in our lives, we will remain stuck in the mire of guilt unable to move forward. Those who are in Christ Jesus are not subject to be slaves to guilt once they have confessed their failures, mistakes, and sin to God. Set free from guilt and condemnation through confession and repentance, we are free in Christ.

God meets us in His love. He gives us the undeserved gift of grace and forgiveness in Jesus Christ. He removes the stigma of guilt that haunts because He took all our guilt on the cross at Calvary and made an end to it.

Today, rise up and accept this gift of God. Choose to be guilt free. You won't ever get rich filling a jar with pennies for every time you condemn yourself in guilt, but you will know God's riches when you allow Him to fill you to overflowing with His forgiveness and grace.

Go Deeper

Guilt is associated with stress, depression, anxiety, and various physical illnesses. What physical and emotional changes have you noticed within you when you have carried guilt in your life?

Guilt is a word that carries a lot of negative weight in meaning. But there are many antonyms for guilt mentioned in the Bible. Name some words that are opposite of guilt. How do you embrace these words in your life to counter the effects of guilt?

The Scripture heading proclaims that there is no condemnation in Christ Jesus. Sometimes our own teens and young adults condemn us when their life choices do not turn out the way they expected. How can you remind yourself that you are not responsible for their choices?

Meditate on Scripture

And he touched my mouth and said: "Behold, this has touched your lips; your guilt is taken away, and your sin atoned for."

Isaiah 6:7 ESV

For all have sinned and fall short of the glory of God.

Romans 3:23 ESV

As far as the east is from the west, so far has he removed our transgressions from us.

Psalm 103:12 NIV

Then I heard a loud voice in heaven say: "Now have come the salvation and the power and the kingdom of our God, and the authority of his Messiah. For the accuser of our brothers and sisters, who accuses them before our God day and night, has been hurled down.

Revelations 12:10 NIV

Pray

Dear Heavenly Father,

When I confess my sins, You are faithful to forgive and purify me from all unrighteousness. My guilt is taken away and my sin atoned for. I thank you that I can walk in freedom from guilt because You have moved all my transgressions as far as the east is from the west. Thank You Lord, because of Your salvation, I do not have to live with guilt from my past mistakes, bad choices, and sin. Through Your kingdom and by Your authority, my accuser, Satan, can no longer hurl accusations and guilt against me. Praise You Father, that guilt was nailed on the cross once and for all.

Amen

"True faith means holding
nothing back.
It means putting every hope
in God's fidelity
to His Promises."

— Francis Chan

HOPELESSNESS

I wait for the LORD, my whole being waits,
and in His Word I put my hope.
Psalm 130:5 NIV

Katie (not her real name) has many mental illnesses and disorders. She was unbearable in her teen years. As time passed, her parents' hope of seeing her life improve with age withered. With their marriage barely hanging on, the rest of the family broke down, too. How much more could they take?

Weary, depressed, and hopeless, Katie's parents didn't expect their family life would be overshadowed by a teen with a multitude of problems. They coped by detaching themselves, both emotionally and mentally.

Katie's parents are not alone. Thousands of parents are confronted with teens heavy into drugs and alcohol. Others are faced with the challenges of porn addiction, eating disorders, suicidal tendencies, and sexual identity crises.

Tackling these issues on a daily basis, parents eventually come to a breaking point. They love their children but are heartbroken over their child's destructive behaviors. Despite their love, their growing weariness and exhaustion results in having nothing else to give. Their struggles are enormous, yet equal to the amount of love they have for their child.

Faith and hope deteriorate when our teen's issues are magnified. Desperate, we look to the world for answers when we don't hear from God right away. In fact, as some parents learn, what the world offers only adds more pain and sorrow instead of hope, healing, and peace.

The Lord understands our limitations and shortcomings. This is why He provided us with unlimited resources of His Word and the power of prayer to build our faith in Him. To encourage our hearts with hope.

> *There is surely a future hope for you, and your hope will not be cut off.*
>
> Proverbs 23:18 NIV

I didn't always receive immediate answers to my prayers. My daughter endured more difficult things as time passed. Even so, in some cases, God allowed our troubling circumstances to teach us life lessons we might not have learned if our teen was well and whole—especially when it came to being steadfast in hope. The hardest part in the process was keeping our faith focused on the Lord and not on our situations as He worked on Daniela.

So how do we keep our hope from waning when all we see is crisis in a hopeless world?

We must remind ourselves of the Lord's promises throughout His Word in every Bible verse with the word "hope." We will be amazed, encouraged, and strengthened in hope as we apply God's Word to our lives. Take it one day at a time—hour by hour, minute by minute, and step by step. Yes, this world overflows in hopelessness, but thank goodness we have a God who reigns supreme with hope, peace, and healing.

> *Wait for the LORD; be strong and take heart and wait for the LORD.*
>
> Psalm 27:14 NIV

This verse encourages us to be strong (courageous) and to take heart (not to lose hope) as we wait upon Him. Even though we cannot see with our earthly eyes what God is doing, we can be assured that our Heavenly Father is always working on our behalf to bring about the fulfillment of His plan for our child no matter how dire it looks. In essence, God is saying, "Don't lose hope! I got this!"

God's everlasting faithfulness never ceases. He will direct us in all things we need to know and shower us with sprinkles of hope and comfort along the way. His grace will sustain us when you lean on Him.

Trust in His Word. Pray His Word. Believe in His Word. These are anchors to keep you steady during unsettling storms and floaters to keep your hope above the waves that try to pull you under. In this way, your period of hopelessness will come to an end as you rejoice to see God work mightily in your family.

Go Deeper

Have you felt hopeless lately with your teen? Read Mark 5:35-42. What did Jesus say to the official? If you were to bring your teen before Jesus and He gave the same reply, what would your response be?

Hope means to trust in, wait for, or expect something good and beneficial will come to you. Christ is our hope. How does the word "Hope" apply to your circumstances?

How can you renew hope in Christ for your family, despite the pain that you are going through during this time of crisis?

Meditate on Scripture

I waited patiently for the LORD; he turned to me and heard my cry.

Psalm 40:1 NIV

Through whom also we have obtained our introduction by faith into this grace in which we stand; and we exult in hope of the glory of God. And not only this, but we also exult in our tribulations, knowing that tribulation brings about perseverance; and perseverance, proven character; and proven character, hope; and hope does not disappoint,

152

because the love of God has been poured out within our hearts through the Holy Spirit who was given to us.

Romans 5:2-5 NIV

Now faith is confidence in what we hope for and assurance about what we do not see.

Hebrews 11:1 NIV

Pray

Dear Heavenly Father,

Restore to me the hope I need to see our family through this crisis. I know You have heard my cry Lord, as I wait patiently for those answers. Help me God, to exalt you not just in my time of rejoicing but also in my time of tribulations. I know Lord, that as I persevere, I will grow more in faith, hope, and endurance. Let these crises build Godly character in me—one of hope—for I know hope does not disappoint. Show me how to soak up Your Word so that I can fend off worry, fear, and hopelessness. Give me a faith that is confident, and a hope that is secure as I daily seek you. And having done ALL, help me to stand!

Amen

"Our real blessings often appear to us in the shape of pains, losses and disappointments; but let us have patience and we soon shall see them in their proper figures."

— Joseph Addison

HURT

Be completely humble and gentle; be patient,
bearing with one another in love.
Ephesians 4:2 NIV

I sat down and cried. How could Daniela do this to me? The never-ending round of crises, destructive behaviors, manipulation, and humiliation grew more severe and difficult to heal from. What did I do to deserve this pain? Did I have a big sign over my head saying, *"Hurt mom. She can take it because she loves unconditionally?"*

Our teens do objectionable things all the time when they are in crisis. They don't think of how crushed we will be by their actions. Teens caught up in a frenzy of emotion and unfettered feelings never think about others in their distress—chiefly those who have loved them most their whole lives. Their brain does not compute the consequences and hurtful ramifications of foolish decisions made, lacking discernment. This is especially true in the world of the "I Want It Now" mentality.

Your teen may think, *I don't care about Mom and Dad's feelings. I don't care if something happens to me because it's my life, not my parents. Mom and Dad will get over it one day. They say they will never stop loving me.* They continue in their negative behaviors of not speaking to you, committing unacceptable actions behind your back, or going over the edge in their antics.

Let's face it—selfishness is the default human condition, often manifesting its worst in the teen and young adult years. In my teen years, a friend once said to me, "I only listen to three other people in my life—Me, Myself, and I." In hindsight, I finally understand why they said this: They were hurting in deep places.

When a person is beset by wrongdoings perpetrated against them, disappointment sets in with painful, traumatic effects. In an effort to protect themselves, even from those they love, the individual nursing hurt feelings builds a wall between them, others, and God.

Does this sound familiar? This hurtful road map was true for my daughter. Her deep hurt caused her to not feel loved, carving a path of disastrous results that not only affected her life, but ours, her parents, as well.

In *Complaint Free Relationships: Transforming Your Life One Relationship at a Time,* author Will Bowen writes, "Hurt people, hurt people." This truth is evident in family dynamics where troubled teens hurt us because they are hurt.

To be gentle, patient, and long-bearing with those who hurt us may seem like a calling above and beyond our ability. Yet, God's love is greater and filled with strength and compassion towards us and our children.

Our Heavenly Father is hurt every day by our actions, whether committed accidentally or on purpose. Still, He continues to reach out to us with unconditional love and forgiveness, even though we don't deserve it. He can empower us to walk our hurt filled paths, exercising this same loving and long-suffering attitude with our children.

The wounds you suffer in your hurt may not fade completely, but the Lord can soften their lasting effects and refresh you with healing.

Go Deeper

God is also a parent, not just over our teens, but us, too. With that in mind, how can you show forgiveness, love, mercy, and grace towards your teen the way Christ has shown for us?

When your hurts consume your heart, they may lead to your own manifesting of negative behaviors such as anger, bitterness, and unforgiveness. What behavioral response are you aware of within yourself when you are hurt? How has responding in such a way influenced you in a negatively?

Assignment: Pray for everyone who has hurt you and ask God how to show compassion and forgiveness toward those who have offended or done wrong to you.

Meditate on Scripture

My soul is weary with sorrow; strengthen me according to your word.

Psalm 119:28 NIV

I consider that our present sufferings are not worth comparing with the glory that will be revealed in us.

Romans 8:18 NIV

In my distress I prayed to the LORD, and the LORD answered me and set me free.

Psalm 118:5 NIV

Pray

Dear Heavenly Father,

When filled with hurt and pain, it is hard to be humble and gentle. My soul is weary with sorrow. My patience dwindles as unforgiveness and sadness grow due to the hurt in my heart. Give me strength, O God, according to Your Word. Because of Your great love for me and my family, I know I will not be consumed by hurt, for Your compassions and faithfulness never fail. They are new to me every morning. May those same compassions be renewed in me and in my child. For I know the present sufferings I feel are not worth the great glory that will be unveiled and revealed in us.

Amen

IMPATIENCE

And let us not grow weary of doing good,
for in due season we will reap, if we do not give up.
Galatians 6:9 ESV

You throw your hands in the air with disgust. You stomp from the room and slam everything in your path. You run to the bathroom, lock the door and let out a scream. You sit in your car and sob onto the steering wheel. Your patience temporarily flies out the window. Welcome to my world!

How much more can a parent take? There are teens that quietly destroy their lives and there are teens that outwardly cause chaos and rebellion at every turn. With our patience already worn thin, one more destructive action by our teen may push us over the edge where we lose it all. Could this be you?

We may be at the police station or before a judge with our teen. We may be on our way to a recovery program, a hospital, or a state mandated correctional facility. Our patience falters when confronted with repeated crises. Do any of us really have enduring patience under this kind of pressure? Only God can so endure.

I often ask myself, "Why does God have so much patience with me?" I believe the patience God demonstrates towards us are love-lessons packed with forgiveness, grace, and mercy. His patience instructs us so we can express this same patience towards our child.

I know this to be true. I have had to ask the Lord to forgive me, show me grace, and grant mercy to me in the midst of our chaotic home conditions. Hurt and broken, my daughter struggled without the ability to filter through her emotional and mental pain. Yet, I expected her to get it together and understand what she needed to do. The old "pick yourself up by the bootstrap" principle didn't work.

Then there is the impatience of not seeing God move in the way we want or as fast as we want. Multiple times I moved ahead when I shouldn't have. I thought I knew best, as if my choices were better than God's. I needed to ask, "Are they?"

The story of Abraham and Sarah in the Book of Genesis illustrates this idea of rushing ahead of God with impatience. Sarah believed God was not moving quick enough to fulfill His promise to her that she would become a mother. In her frustration, she gave her slave girl, Hagar, over to Abraham so that a child could be conceived through her. This was in keeping with a prevalent cultural practice of the day. Sarah decided to control her own destiny for motherhood in a timelier manner, in her own strength and worldly wisdom.

Hagar gave Abraham the son he had hoped for and ridiculed Sarah for not being able to conceive. Sarah's plan backfired. It brought pain and stirred anger because she wasn't willing to wait on the Lord.

I don't know about you, but when I make a plan in my own strength without God's support, it usually backfires, too. The Lord makes plans according to His will and our welfare. When we get ahead of what the Lord wants for us, we stand to lose out on His blessings for us and our family. In our disobedience, not willing to wait on the Lord with patience, life-altering consequences can and do happen. Behaving out of an impatient spirit may affect our marriage, our finances, our spiritual life, and our teen in negative ways.

Sarah learned a bitter lesson during the years of ridicule because of the slave girl's child. She got ahead of God's perfect will for her. Her plan did not work out as she'd thought. If only she had waited on God for His plans. Still, in due season according to His purpose and promise, the God of forgiveness, grace, and mercy blessed Sarah with a son named Isaac.

These days, persistence pays off. I refuse to give up. I can't do it all in my own strength, I ask for help, guidance, and wisdom from family, spiritual authority, and dear friends. I do not want to produce hasty results acting in impatience anymore. This requires humility mixed with patience and a lot of prayer.

Don't be an impatient Sarah. Wait. Wait patiently for the Lord. Doing so will be a clear affirmation of your trust and faith in Him to keep you through any storm that comes your way.

Go Deeper

 Was there a time in which you felt you could no longer be patient with your teen in crisis? Write about how you wanted to respond, how you did respond, and what the consequences were because of your response. What did you learn from this?

 Write about a decision you have made without God's guidance. Did you regret not waiting on the Lord's counsel? Did you ask God to forgive you? How did He show you His grace and mercy afterward?

 What are some ways in which you can turn your impatience around to patience?

Meditate on Scripture

But they soon forgot what he had done and did not wait for his plan to unfold.

Psalm 106:13 NIV

Wait for the LORD; be strong and take heart and wait for the LORD.

Psalm 27:14 NIV

The LORD will fight for you; you need only to be still.

Exodus 14:14 NI

Pray

Dear Heavenly Father,

My disobedience has caused heartache. I grew weary of waiting and gave up on Your plan, Lord. Please forgive me for not listening. Because of my sin, I know there are consequences that I must face. Lord, help me to repent and have mercy on me. Give me patience to get through each situation and crisis in my life. Although I may suffer for a while, I know it produces perseverance. Help me to remain faithful in Your restoration and healing of my family. As You fight for me, I will be still. When I start to stray and go back to my old ways, remind me of Sarah's poor choices and judgment. Show me how to wait for Your perfect plan to unfold.

Amen

"God knows our situation;
He will not judge us
as if we had no difficulties
to overcome.
What matters is the sincerity
and perseverance of our will
to overcome them."

— C.S. Lewis

JUDGMENT

Do not judge, or you too will be judged. For in the same way you judge others, you will be judged, and with the measure you use, it will be measured to you.
Matthew 7:1-2 NIV

The gavel slammed down announcing the order of judgment. Guilty!

There it was. In big, black bold letters:

"You are a terrible mother and you should be ashamed of yourself for how you are raising your daughter."

Those were the words I received in a two-page long email criticizing my parenting. It left me angry, upset, and defensive. On the one hand, I didn't blame this woman for how she felt. After all, only weeks earlier I made some very strong statements about her child, a flood of critical words spoken out of exasperation. I judged her parenting based on what I saw that I didn't like, perhaps as a result of dealing with my own failures as a parent.

Let's face facts. No one likes to be judged. Many parents feel more vulnerable to judgment and criticism when they have a teen in crisis. The field of judges leveling gavels is broad, consisting of peers, authority figures, family members, and even those of scant acquaintance.

Sometimes judgment comes from someone who lacks understanding about your situation and doesn't care to ask. This may cause you to take offense and discount their words.

I admit, I needed to really hear the truth about my parenting, but when critical words came my way, all I could hear was judgment leaking through.

When we hit rock bottom, our emotions are a poor lens through which to view life or trust our feelings. A constant stream of inadequacy, embarrassment, shame, guilt, and failure assaulted me regularly. I often wore these emotions like the latest fashion. Being fully clothed in these pesky, inaccurate thoughts, seemed natural. Adding judgment as the latest accessory to my wardrobe of emotions seemed just what my ensemble needed to be complete.

While all these emotions swirled around and tore me apart, my heart ached for compassion, understanding, and support. With my ongoing struggle wallowing in shame, I feared how others viewed me. Over and over, my parenting skills seemed microscopically enlarged for all to see my failures and mistakes.

Eventually, I became defensive and angry. I

expected criticism to automatically come from anyone who talked to me—or didn't talk to me—especially other parents. I accepted their stares and wordless actions as rejection. I noticed a withdrawal of fellowship from others. No one wanted to be around me and it became clear that parents did not want to have my daughter around their children either.

As time passed, the anger I carried ignited into a fire of bitterness. Because I felt judged, I believed I had the right to be angry and judge others in return. This only encouraged my choice to openly criticize whomever I perceived as criticizing me.

Unforgiveness crept in and its effects only hurt myself and my family. It also inhibited the power and effectiveness of my prayers. I knew the Bible taught that in order for our prayers to be answered, we must get rid of a judgmental heart through the act of forgiveness and repentance.

What is wrong with me? The thought nagged me daily and the conviction of God lay heavy on my heart. How could I leave room for God to heal my heart and our broken home if I continued to look for the faults in others and judge them? Did I perceive things unjustly because of the attitude of my heart? Was I in sin for being angry? Could I show forgiveness from my heart the way Christ forgave me—humbly sacrificing self?

It was obvious from the Lord's conviction that my

behavior was sinful. I knew this saddened God's heart and that my words and actions towards others may have hurt them just as deep. The truth of this broke me in godly sorrow and convinced me of my need to repent.

In hindsight, from the first I should have fallen on my knees and prayed for these families, especially those who were in similar crisis. I was the perfect candidate to understand their hurts and brokenness. Unfortunately, the companion sins of fear and pride infected my heart. I chose not to pray for those I thought had judged me. Instead of offering encouraging words and compassion to them, I chose to judge them—the very thing that tortured me.

I slowly realized why I tended to excuse my false thinking that I had the right to judge others. Was it a reaction to an already deep hurt dwelling within? Was I protecting myself from being hurt again or was it a defense mechanism to some truth I didn't want to address? In either case, I needed to take it to the throne room of God to find those answers, perhaps asking first what David asked when he became aware of his sin in Psalm 51:10 NKJV—"*Create in me a clean heart, O, God.*"

How do we stop a judgmental attitude within ourselves towards others? We need the Holy Spirit's help to remind us of God's Word in Proverbs 19:11 NIV: "*A person's wisdom yields patience; it is to one's glory to overlook an offense.*"

And again, in Matthew 18:15 NIV: "*If your brother*

or sister sins, go and point out their fault, just between the two of you. If they listen to you, you have won them over."

God encourages us in these verses to be patient with others and quick to show compassion and mercy towards them. Often people who judge do so because they are not fully informed or understand the issues beyond what they see. Countless times I have sat down with the one who judged and shared with them a small portion of what Daniela was enduring. They had no idea of the things she suffered from and the diagnosis' that we were addressing. By the time they left, they were in tears, asking me for forgiveness.

So how can you overcome your feelings of being judged? Here's a simple checklist to start:

- Choose to ask God to bless the person you feel has judged you in order to be free from the weight of being judged.
- Keep your focus on Christ, not on what others say, who judge by sight and not understanding. Your defense is Christ who sees and knows all.
- Ask the Lord to protect your heart, not only from the judgment of others, but also to keep you from judging in return.

Going Deeper

 How can you demonstrate care and support without being judgmental?

The feeling that you are being judged can also invite other types of emotions such as anger and hurt. What other emotions are you experiencing from being judged? How can you turn those emotions over to God?

 From the Scripture in Matthew 18:15 above, how can we, in a Godly and gentle way, correct the one who offended us?

Meditate on Scripture

Do nothing out of selfish ambition or vain conceit. Rather, in humility value others above yourselves, not looking to your own interests but each of you to the interests of the others.

Philippians 2:3-4 NIV

Why do you look at the speck of sawdust in your brother's eye and pay no attention to the plank in your own eye? How can you say to your brother, 'Let me take the speck out of your eye,' when all the time there is a plank in your own eye? You hypocrite! First take the plank out of your own eye, and then you will see clearly to remove the speck from your brother's eye.

Matthew 7:3-5 NIV

Pray

Dear Heavenly Father,

I am sorry for the anger and unforgiveness that I have held within my heart. Enable me to be patient and to show God-like humility towards others and not focus on what I may think is an offense. Clear out the negative thoughts within me that come from receiving and perceiving judgment. When I am quick to point out someone's faults, show me where I need to be corrected instead. Change my attitude to show mercy in which your Word says triumphs over judgment. Cause me to be humble and mindful of others and their struggles. Remind me, Lord, that I am accountable to You for my actions. Let me not put a stumbling block or hindrance in the way of my fellow brothers and sisters. Give me a heart to extend grace and love towards others who are hurting as much as I am.

Amen

"Faith is the deliberate confidence in the character of God whose ways you may not understand at the time."

— Oswald Chambers

LONELINESS

The LORD himself goes before you and will be with you;
he will never leave you nor forsake you.
Do not be afraid; do not be discouraged.
Deuteronomy 31:8 NIV

Escape. Withdraw. Detach. This was my world when threatened by outsiders wanting to see into my broken family's life. I ran in the opposite direction from them.

At first it felt uncomfortable to withdraw, especially from other Christians at church, as if I was doing something wrong. Being involved in church and serving in ministry, I believed the unwritten rule to never step down from a ministry or leave the fellowship. Even so, my escape became my solace. Comforted in my flight, I detached myself completely from others so they wouldn't have the opportunity to nose into my life or that of my child.

While Daniela wrestled through multiple crises, I didn't want to deal with anyone. When I heard a hurtful comment, I shut down inside and found ways to retreat from the confrontation. As problems continued, I isolated myself from everyone and everything. I could stand in a room full of people and yet distance myself from them all, both mentally and physically. This is how I once survived my personal and emotional storms.

My daughter's issues multiplied daily. One day she talked about death and the desire to hurt others beside herself. Another day she wanted to bleach her skin because she hated the color of it. A week might pass and she'd threaten to run away. She constantly hacked the passwords on my computers and viewed sites about satanism, gypsy cultures, subcultures, self-harm, and a plethora of other destructive issues. It was never ending.

The destructive influence of these topics surfaced outwardly in the words she spoke to scare others, especially other parents. They questioned and accused us in their fear and concern. No one seemed able to understand the depth of pain we felt in our tortured bubble.

During a self-harming incident, I asked my daughter to find new ways to cope with her pain and hurt. I encouraged writing on her body instead of cutting, which my peers frowned upon. I painted her room with chalkboard black paint and told her to write whatever she wanted as long as she didn't cut herself. Finally, I asked her to take my camera and use her creativity to express her brokenness through pictures. Not long after, I received a call from a family member that someone from the church had seen her social media filled with dark and disturbing images. They didn't seem to understand why I was okay with this.

Lonely, inside my bubble, I secured myself from their questions and opinions.

Later, after speaking to two different psychologists, I learned I was doing a good thing. These outside-the-box suggestions shocked my peers but gave my daughter the opportunity to express herself in safe ways for herself and for others.

At the time, no one understood this. Fearing more negative judgment, I withdrew further from everyone.

By this point, one or two missed gatherings turned into many. Gone were the days of outings with friends for coffee or the movies. It became increasingly clear that we lived our lives differently because of my daughter's difficulties and my struggle to get by each day.

Eventually, I chose to remain in contact with others through phone or email, allowing me a form of control over who I let into my bubble and who I kept out. The problem with this self-imposed isolation was my growing indifference to hear the advice of others or to fellowship with them.

Loneliness and depression consumed me.

All I wanted was my child to be fixed. We couldn't afford counselors at the time and she refused to open up to the ones that did offer help. In frustration, my poor choices added to our despair as my need to control kept her from getting real help. My isolation bubble enlarged like a giant fenced wall surrounding me. It pushed others out and locked me in its vacuum center with my sole companion, Loneliness.

I saw no hope. I didn't feel God. But, somehow, I knew He was there. Somewhere.

God knows isolation from others is not beneficial. His Word points out the importance of fellowship with others in 1 Corinthians 12:26-27 NIV saying, *"If one part suffers, every part suffers with it; if one part is honored, every part rejoices with it. Now you are the body of Christ, and each of you is a member of it."*

I thought it was a good thing to be alone, to retreat and detach. I thought it would keep me focused on the most important thing—my daughter. Unknowingly, I did the opposite. I pushed family, friends, and the church away, and in so doing, I pushed away the One who could help me the most—GOD, the Father.

If I shut the door to Him, how could He help? The invisible fenced walls that guarded me did not heal, support, or provide freedom for Daniela. Instead, they only locked me away from the real help we needed. I knew the consequences of remaining there would be disastrous. Weary, my emotions unraveled with feelings of depression and thoughts of suicide. My fences needed to come down and my bubble needed to burst for there to be change in me and my family.

If I wanted God to restore our broken family, I had to allow Him, along with trusted brothers and sisters in Christ, back into my life. Back into our lives. As a family, we needed the Body of Christ to walk with us through our storm so we wouldn't feel alone. Unlocking the door of faith is necessary for us to get out of the closet of loneliness. We need not fear or feel alone when we have God leading us on our road of faith. To not do so proves we do not have trust in God.

I chose to let go of my loneliness and collapse the fence surrounding me. I allowed God to replace it with His refuge of hope, fellowship, and support. This meant trusting God's wisdom as to the direction for our family and trusting other Christ followers to hold us up without judgment or condemnation.

Don't erect boundaries of isolation or loneliness. Allow God to bring others into your life to minister, uplift, and encourage you in your time of distress. If you can't find the necessary direct and in-person support, refer to the resources included in the back of this book. Let God unlock the doors of your fence of loneliness.

Go Deeper

 Proverbs 18:1 ESV says, *"Whoever isolates himself seeks his own desire; he breaks out against all sound judgment."* Why is it wrong to isolate yourself?

 Personal Challenge: Listen to the song, *I Am Not Alone,* by Kari Jobe. Write down all the things that God does for you when you feel alone and how you can respond.

 What are some ways that God shows you He has not forsaken or left you in your time of loneliness?

Meditate on Scripture

The LORD God said, "It is not good for the man to be alone. I will make a helper suitable for him."

Genesis 2:18 NIV

Yet I am always with you; you hold me by my right hand.

Psalm 73:23 NIV

You are my hiding place; you will protect me from trouble and surround me with songs of deliverance.

Psalm 32:7 NIV

Pray

Dear Heavenly Father,

Forgive me for withdrawing from You and those who truly love me and my family and want the best for us. I chose to hide away and hoped my problems would disappear. I was in denial. Today, I choose to not give up and isolate myself in loneliness. I choose to seek out others to encourage and support me and my family in our need. Lord, I recognize that I am one of many parts called according to Your purposes and that You may use me one day to help others. I want to be refreshed and learn from Your Word so what I learn from my life experiences can be used as a blessing to encourage and support others. Guide my steps so each person I encounter will be blessed by You. Comfort me in knowing that I am not alone, for You are with me.

Amen

PLIABILITY

Then the word of the Lord came to me. He said, "Can I not do with you, Israel, as this potter does?" declares the Lord. "Like clay in the hand of the potter, so are you in my hand, Israel."
Jeremiah 18:5-6 NIV

When I was a kid, Silly Putty and Play Dough were the best toys ever—a pure delight to play with. Unfortunately, after continued use they dried out, got dirty, and became unusable.

What I liked the most about playing with them were the various shapes I could mold them into. With Silly Putty, I copied images like cartoons from newspapers then stretched the images out as far as possible. The distorted picture ignited hysterical laughter every time.

As I aged, I discovered another moldable art product: clay. Like Silly Putty and Play Dough, clay must stay moist to remain moldable. Although there are differences between the two, such as usage, stability, and strength, the end result, after some time, remained the same: they all dried out, got dirty and became unpliable.

As a parent with a teen in crisis, when my spiritual life dried out due to my weakness, I became less flexible and moldable. Like clay, Silly Putty, or Play Dough left out of its container, stiff like a rock and difficult to revive, there was little for God to work with.

We harden in the wrong way when our teen is in constant crisis. We rarely keep ourselves pliable, moistened through God's Word and prayer. I'll be honest, it's a hard thing to stay malleable in the Lord when I'm too tired to pray, don't want to worship, and am not in the mood to be thankful.

I learned a valuable lesson over the years: be pliable in God's plan of action. I gave up my way of doing things and put my hard-headed attitude and pride aside, allowing God to move through our situation.

The stretching required wasn't as simple as Silly Putty. I needed to be flexible with the counselor's advice and open to having things exposed that were uncomfortable to talk about. Truly, the counselor has heard everything. My story—or for that matter, your story—will not be a surprise.

When the potter begins to work with clay the way God works with us, he has an end product goal in mind. He begins with kneading all the air pockets out of the clay with pressure, so the clay won't burst or crumble when placed in the fire of the kiln. Then, he lays a strong, firm foundation upon which he adds layers and layers to strengthen it and raise it up into a useful vessel. The more I leaned into the Lord, the more I gained layers of hope, growth, and strength.

The most difficult alterations in my life came during the purification process—all that heavy kneading and pounding out of air pockets. If a potter sees a flaw in the clay as he builds, he must start over from the beginning. He crushes the clay before trying to mold and layer it anew. When the potter is finished, the vessel he created must be glazed and baked at a high temperature to become strong and useful.

My life is a metaphor of this process of being molded over and over, layer upon layer, then glazed in the Holy Spirit, and burned in fire for strength. My life had to be transformed in order for God to bring restoration.

God is not finished with me. He continues to refine me in other areas of my life until He sees that my foundation is layered in the right way. Now, every day when I wake up as a transformed vessel from the Potter's hands, I choose to thank God for one thing in my life. Sometimes the severity of our troubles overwhelms me. I might not be able to pray anything more than, "Jesus, help me." That is enough. My God is there by my side. And when I have no energy to worship, I listen to the ministry of music and meditate on the words. God understands. He sees me.

He sees you, too. He knows you are dried up right

now, perhaps feeling dirty, and completely unusable. He wants to mold and transform your life towards restoration. Allow Him be the Potter in your life. Be pliable enough to begin the process by thanking God for one thing every day. Just pray, "Jesus, help me." Tune into worship with a listening heart and meditate on the words spilling over and into you. When you allow yourself to be stretched by doing those simple things, your heart and spirit will be revived once again.

Go Deeper

 God desired to mold Israel like a potter molds clay, as mentioned in Jeremiah 18. But Israel was hard-hearted and inflexible in His hands. God had many plans for Israel and they missed out on the blessings because of the sin of stubbornness. Do you find yourself having those same attitudes when it comes to change? Express how you respond to the idea of bending to change and transformation in your life.

 Looking back, what areas of your life have you experienced growth from being pliable? What areas were you not willing to bend in and why?

 How does God want you to be pliable for Him and your situation with your teen?

Meditate on Scripture

For it is God who works in you to will and to act in order to fulfill his good purpose.

Philippians 2:13 NIV

The works of his hands are faithful and just; all his precepts are trustworthy.

Psalm 111:7 NIV

Listen to advice and accept instruction, that you may gain wisdom in the future.

Proverbs 19:20 ESV

Let the wise hear and increase in learning, and the one who understands obtain guidance.

Proverbs 1:5 ESV

Pray

Dear Heavenly Father,

Forgive me for my stubbornness in not wanting to be pliable and molded into the parent you want me to be. Lord, I repent from my disobedience and ask for Your forgiveness. Begin to make me into the vessel of honor You want me to be for I know that when You work in me, it is to fulfill Your good purpose. Reveal to me how to be flexible according to Your plans. Let me heed Your advice, accept instruction, increase in learning, and gain wisdom. Mold our broken family and make it stronger. Guide me again with Your Holy Spirit as I seek you through Your Word and in prayer. The works of Your hands are faithful and just and all Your precepts are trustworthy.

Amen

"If you can't fly, then run,
If you can't run, then walk,
If you can't walk, then crawl,
but whatever you do,
you have to keep
moving forward."

— Martin Luther King Jr

POWERLESSNESS

We also pray that you will be strengthened with
all his glorious power so you will have
all the endurance and patience you need.
Colossians 1:11 NLT

You're the parent who rushed your teen to the hospital from an overdose. You're the parent who discovered signs of a bulimic disorder in your teen. You're the parent who is in a panic state because your teen just ran away for the third time and could be in danger. You're the parent who feels powerless in the face of such crises.

I felt powerless when I couldn't stop Daniela from cutting. I felt powerless when she snuck out of the house in the middle of the night to see friends. I felt powerless when she got into some legal trouble and ended up in juvenile court. I felt powerless when she almost died from a laced drug. I felt powerless when she wanted to commit suicide. I felt powerless when she was in the depths of deep depression, anxiety, and Post-Traumatic Stress Disorder.

How in the world can we find endurance and hope when we feel powerless?

When the punch of powerlessness hits you, you wonder how to begin to deal with the latest crisis. Like one of those wild amusement rides, you don't know what direction you are heading or when you will get off. But you had better buckle up! And when you finally do get off, you struggle to stand on two feet overcome by a swarm of dizzy perpetrated by an unsettling dilemma.

No matter how much you try, the fact is, you are powerless. God understands when we feel powerless, helpless, and weak. His power is far beyond our human ability to comprehend. Yet, through Jesus Christ, we have free access to His power in our lack. He knows exactly how much we need and when we need it.

He knows exactly what is happening with our son or daughter in crisis, too, so the power He gives will meet their essential need. Psalm 139 tells us that God knew your child before they were even born. He knew them through their carefree joys as a very young child in the innocent years, and knows them now, better than you do, since they have embarked on the road of dangerous and destructive behaviors. He also knows, intimately, the pain this has caused you. He has watched mankind walk that destructive path since the Fall.

Thankfully, God knows how to reach our children when we are not able to. This is the loving God we serve. We can have confidence in Him knowing He is aware of where our child is, what they are doing, and how to heal them at the center of their need.

Nothing is outside of God's knowledge or power to exercise on our behalf. Our job is to simply and consistently bring our troubled teen and their problems to His feet through prayer. Then, stand in faith, even if it is the size of a mustard seed. God will give us the power to take the next step.

For me, I often thought my mustard seed of faith had been ground to dust and not a seed anymore. Even still, I relied on my Heavenly Father—a Power able to keep me in my weakness.

So, when you feel powerless, reach for His Word. There is courage, patience, wisdom, and peace written on every page. His spoken Word will inspire and lift you up to get through each day. Lean on others for support and prayer. When two or more are together in His name, be assured, He will answer. This is His promise to us. His power enlarges and prevails.

Oh, my Great and Mighty God, nothing is too difficult for thee!

Go Deeper

Powerlessness is not a weakness. It is the state of not being able to step in and fix the situation. Mark 5:21-24 NASB reminds us of the power we have access to when we reach out for Jesus: *When Jesus had crossed over again in the boat to the other side, a large crowd gathered around Him; and so He stayed by the seashore. One of the synagogue officials named Jairus came up, and on seeing Him, fell at His feet and implored Him earnestly, saying, "My little daughter is at the point of death; please come and lay Your hands on her, so that she will get well and live."* This father was powerless and couldn't help his child. He fully admitted his inability while boldly petitioning Jesus to exercise His ability. We are in the same position. The father in this story knew exactly who to go to for power to change his situation. Who do you seek out with the power to change your situation? Think about the great faith this powerless father exhibited to seek out Jesus Christ for help. How does his story increase your faith? In light of this father's decision to seek out Jesus, was he really as powerless as he thought he was?

What does the following verse say about the power that is in us: *The Spirit of God, who raised Jesus from the dead, lives in you. And just as God raised Christ Jesus from the dead, he will give life to your mortal bodies by this same Spirit living within you.* Romans 8:11 NLT

Meditate on Scripture

The LORD is my strength and my shield; my heart trusts in him, and he helps me.

Psalm 28:7 NIV

LORD, be gracious to us; we long for you. Be our strength every morning, our salvation in time of distress.

Isaiah 33:2 NIV

The righteous cry, and the LORD hears and delivers them out of all their troubles. The LORD is near to the brokenhearted and saves those who are crushed in spirit.

Psalm 34:17-18 NIV

Pray

Dear Heavenly Father,

I feel powerless to help my teen/young adult in their crisis. You said that when we call upon Your Name, You will hear us when we call. Lord, be my strength in this time of need. Shield me from the attacks of the enemy that are determined to keep me powerless. My heart cries out to trust in You and You alone. Be gracious, O Lord, as I seek You every morning for Your strength. Thank you for being my salvation in times of distress. I praise You that You are always there to deliver me in my troubles. You uplift me when I feel brokenhearted and crushed in my spirit. Thank you for Your provision that sustains me during my time of powerlessness, hurt, and pain.

Amen

"God's work done
in God's way
will never lack
God's supplies."

— Hudson Taylor

PRIDE

Though the LORD is great, he cares for the humble,
but he keeps his distance from the proud.
Psalm 138:6 NLT

Most of us would agree that being prideful is not our problem. Not like some really prideful characters we read about in the Bible such as Pharaoh of Egypt, Haman in the book of Esther, and King Saul.

I never thought of myself as a prideful person. Then, one day it hit me: I was filled with pride. Not the confidence kind of pride—but the Pharaoh, Haman, and King Saul kind of pride.

Prior to this epiphany, I kept active in church and had a well-adjusted social life. I was an organized leader, punctual, a good delegator, and strong administrator. All of that swirled down the drain once depression confronted me with a daughter spiraling out of control.

When Daniela's critical issues flared up, a prideful defense mechanism also reared its ugly head in me. I intended to handle Daniela's issues all by myself.

Intervention or counsel was for other parents, not me. At least those were my thoughts at the time.

I prided myself on how quickly I bounced back and recovered from personal challenges in the past. So why couldn't I do this now? I thought of myself as a conqueror and overcomer. In my mindset, getting the best of Daniela's problems was no different. Why on earth would I let someone else call the shots to help our family, especially with my daughter? I was the parent. It's my job. Pride manifested in my life in varied ways:

- Keeping others from counseling me or my daughter
- Counseling my own daughter when I didn't have specialized training and knew nothing of that profession
- Trying to help other parents with their kids problems when I hadn't even fixed my own child's problems
- Thinking I knew it all, could handle things on my own, and do a better job than even God in helping my daughter

This plan of mine didn't last long and didn't fix the problems. They persisted. My family remained broken. My daughter grew darker, wounded and suffering.

Pride doesn't allow us to blame ourselves. So then, who might be at fault for all our troubles?

I admit it—I believed the lie that God gave up on us

and that He didn't care. In actuality, it was the other way around. I stopped caring about what God thought when my pride took over. I couldn't see beyond the huge blind spot my pride had become for me.

Doors to healing and aid for my family appeared closed off to me. Growing aware of the true nature of the crisis, my spirit awakened to what I was doing. Conviction revealed my prideful nature. I needed to admit my sin and ask God for forgiveness. Humility called me to my knees. Instead of wallowing in pride keeping God at a distance, I chose to allow God to take the lead. It was hard at first. To let go of my control was scary, as if someone had blinded me before seating me behind the steering wheel of a car on a racetrack speed course.

When pride takes a front seat in your life, foolish behavior follows. In the Old Testament, a Levite name Uzzah was one of the Israelites tasked with transporting the Ark of God to its new destination. The Ark was Holy and God gave detailed instructions to King David and the Israelites on how to move it with only two rules:

- **Number One:** Do not touch it.
- **Number Two:** Do not look upon the Ark—it was covered and too holy to gaze upon.

Enroute in the convoy, the cart that carried the Ark stumbled in the road. It didn't fall but certainly had a bumpy ride for a few moments. Uzzah immediately stepped in, taking hold of the Ark to stop it from falling. He touched it. The very thing he knew not to do.

Did he believe God needed his help or that God couldn't handle a few bumps in the road? Uzzah knew the death penalty was decreed for rules disobeyed. But it seems he thought the Ark would not make it without his assistance. He thought he could handle things just as good as God—if not better. His pride got in the way.

If we permit pride to take our family in the wrong direction, we invite strong, possibly dire, ramifications. Isn't it better to submit to God, seek forgiveness, draw on humility, and call on God's wisdom when our life stumbles on bumpy roads? Lay aside pride and see God work in your life as well as your teen.

Go Deeper

 Humility is not always easy, but pride is more painful in the end. Knowing this, what avenue will you take from this point forward to get support and help for your family?

 Have you ever felt a distance between you and God because of pride? How can you let go of that pride and draw nearer to Him?

 In Proverbs 16:18 God tells us that pride goes before a fall. What kind of consequences can you suffer when allowing pride first place in attitude and behavior and what will you do to change it?

Meditate on Scripture

The pride of your heart has deceived you, you who live in the clefts of the rocks and make your home on the heights, you who say to yourself, 'Who can bring me down to the ground?'

Obadiah 1:3 NIV

But after Uzziah became powerful, his pride led to his downfall. He was unfaithful to the LORD his God, and entered the temple of the LORD to burn incense on the altar of incense.

2 Chronicles 26:16 NIV

When pride comes, then comes disgrace, but with humility comes wisdom.

Proverbs 11:2 NIV

Pray

Dear Heavenly Father,

Forgive me for allowing pride to inhabit my life and deceive me. Break down the walls of pride so humility rules my heart and Your wisdom guides my mind and spirit. When my fleshly pride tries to control my ways, may I quickly repent before it becomes my downfall, like Uzzah. Squash my controlling spirit and change the attitude of my heart. Instill in me meekness and obedience to follow Your will. By doing so, I will see the blessings and spiritual fruit I so desire.

Amen

"The Christian life is not a constant high. I have my moments of deep discouragement. I have to go to God in prayer with tears in my eyes, and say, 'O God, forgive me' or 'Help me.'"

— Billy Graham

REJECTION

*Come to him, a living stone rejected by men
but in the sight of God chosen and precious.*
1 Peter 2:4 ESV

Have you ever been chosen last when teams were picked for a game? Did you think you were precious to your friends only to feel left out when your name was left off an invitation list to a party? If so, you have probably felt dismissed, rebuffed, abandoned, and yes, rejected.

As our daughter's issues with abandonment and rejection grew, my long-time friendships dwindled away as well. My friends did not understand the severity of our situation; especially if they didn't share the experience of a wayward teen. As much as they wanted to help, they did not know how to respond. Instead they chose to quietly remove themselves from our lives.

As time passed, this rejection started to wear down my heart. I felt shunned when going to church, which quenched my joy. I cynically wondered why I should even go in the first place. Some of our more courageous friends tried to offer help, but because of my hurt and tender

197

emotional state, I chose to allow only a select few into our personal lives. Perhaps those I didn't allow near me felt rejected, too.

Rejection played a major part in my life, from childhood through the teen years. Growing up as an awkward child, I didn't have many friends. By my teens, my self-esteem plummeted. When corrected, my self-worth sunk so low that I didn't care about myself anymore. After multiple hurts and a destabilizing crisis at a young age, I accepted rejection by others as the normal way of things. It hung like a black cloud over my life.

Years later, when I needed support during varied trials with my troubled teen, I expected rejection, and helped it along by pushing people away. This left me with a double dose of pain and hurt.

These personal experiences helped me understand why my daughter struggled in the same way, being abandoned at birth, rejected by peers, and discriminated against by authority figures. Those within her ethnic heritage rejected her because, in their culture, you are considered an outcast if you do not stay within your birth family. In addition, she experienced bullying at a young age, even by those within the Church. But no adult—not even me—knew about these incidents until she revealed them through counseling.

Family crises often stir up painful, forgotten memories. Episodic recollections of past rejection in childhood can rise to the surface, making it difficult to address similar issues in a current situation. We would like to put these memories in the warehouse of our mind and never think about them again. But God may choose to shine His light upon them, in a new season of life, to deal with them once and for all.

Jesus faced rejection many times in his earthly ministry. Perhaps His most painful moment of rejection occurred when His disciples, whom He loved and hand picked as part of His inner circle, denied Him in His most critical time of need—His passion and death. How did Jesus deal with this level of rejection?

He did nothing—yet He did everything.

Jesus modeled divine mercy and forgiveness to rise above rejection. He ignored the taunts and the betrayal and focused on obeying His Heavenly Father's call to the cross. He did not speak a word in His defense. He loved those who spurned Him even unto death. For the joy that was set before Him, He chose purpose over personal pain.

How can we, in the face of rejection and our fragile humanity, show this same level of grace, mercy, and forgiveness towards others?

We can seek to follow Christ's example—choosing to rise above the effects of rejection in our lives when we focus on the joy of our purpose in Him. Certainly, we can choose to hold onto the marks of hurtful episodes from past/present rejections. But isn't it greater to make a joyful exchange of painful rejection for grace, mercy, and forgiveness as won for us by Jesus Christ through His death and resurrection?

Our purpose in Jesus Christ trumps the pain of rejection. We don't have to live with it as a companion. Ask yourself these questions: Which option brings you life and healing? Which option brings peace to quiet your mind and spirit?

Christ's death on the cross crucified rejection. We are no longer subjected to its mark on our lives. The work of Jesus, once and for all, washes that mark of rejection away by His grace. He set a divine example for us to follow. We must not allow rejection to govern our thoughts and emotions.

Thankfully, God does not leave us alone in our frail human nature to try to follow Christ's example with no help. Instead, He gives us the power of the Holy Spirit, our Helper and Comforter, to fight against destructive feelings when they attack us. In His strength we can have victory over rejection. In our weakness, He is strong!

The next time you feel rejected by man, whether through an action of a peer, a friend, or your child, think of Christ who intimately knew what it was to be rejected. He nailed it to a cross, left it there, and rose up to new life free of its stain. Freedom trumps feelings every time.

Go Deeper

 List some of the times that Jesus experienced rejection as recorded in the Bible. How did He guard against responding in anger and bitterness due to rejection?

 You can choose to accept, or reject, rejection in your life. How will you respond when rejection seeks to captivate your emotions?

Describe how it feels to know that you are chosen by and precious to God.

Meditate on Scripture

He came to his own people, and even they rejected him.

John 1:11 NLT

The Spirit himself testifies with our spirit that we are God's children.

Romans 8:16 NIV

Those who know your name trust in you, for you, LORD, have never forsaken those who seek you.

Psalm 9:10 NIV

Pray

Dear Heavenly Father,

I am so thankful that I am not alone when I am faced with rejection. You loved the world so much that You gave

Your only Son, Jesus, on the cross in the midst of many who rejected Him, even His own people. Thank You for Your precious love for us as Your children. We are assured that whatever rejection we face we can identify with You in our time of suffering. Father, please forgive me for focusing on my rejection instead of You. Help me to break free of negative thoughts of rejection. Bring others into my life that will support and uplift me as well as be compassionate to my circumstances. Encourage and comfort me this day as I lean on the Holy Spirit and trust in You Lord, for You will not forsake me.

Amen

REPENTANCE

Whoever heeds discipline shows the way to life,
but whoever ignores correction leads others astray.
Proverbs 10:17 NIV

In denying the true extent of my daughter's troubles, I developed a habit of enabling. Because I did not set boundaries in her life, Daniela ended up in a dangerous situation. She became involved with a group of people who did not have her best interests at heart. They were daring and rebellious, believing they were above the law.

God asked me to obey the wisdom of His Word regarding the discipline and healthy boundaries a parent has a responsibility to set in their children's lives. I chose not to obey Him, continuing my enabling behaviors. I allowed her to build relationships with inappropriate companions. Even my husband, as the head of our household, asked me to set boundaries and hold Daniela accountable. But I did not. I followed after my own heart.

In time, I realized my error when the situation grew out of hand. However, I didn't immediately fall to my knees with a repentant heart and confess where I had gone wrong. But, after serious discussion with my husband, we decided to pray every morning asking God to intervene in our daughter's life. We asked God to do whatever was necessary to remove the negative influences in our daughter's life at any cost.

There's a saying: *Be careful of what you pray for.*

Daniela didn't realize the severity of her situation until it was too late. By that time, she was too deeply entrenched in a life or death game and didn't know how to get out. She did not understand the impact others could have in her life for destruction.

The wake-up call that shocked me out of dependence on myself and my wisdom came the day I found myself at the police station watching my daughter being booked for a crime and locked up. I did not see her again until the court date when we were appointed a public defender. His words nearly brought me to the floor in anguish. "This is serious," he said. "Your daughter may be looking at twenty years in prison for this crime. I don't have much hope that they will be lenient."

That day changed my life.

Though our daughter made destructive choices of her own, I bore responsibility because I am the parent. I could have prevented certain situations from happening. But, I didn't. I disobeyed clear direction from God and disregarded the wisdom of my husband, paying a huge cost.

Because of my disobedience, I set my daughter up for failure. The consequences were severe; the outcome troubling and burdensome. I cried for days. A lack of trust fractured my marriage and affected my relationship with the Lord.

Broken inside and fully convicted of my part in allowing the situation to balloon to this critical point, I finally fell before the Lord in repentance. I took full responsibility for not following through with what God had shown me to do, confirmed through my husband. In humiliation and godly sorrow, I asked both God and my husband to forgive me.

Suffering the painful effects in the aftermath of my disobedience taught me a powerful lesson. God's direction through His Word protects us when we obey it. His wisdom brings wholeness and healing—not heartache. The Lord doesn't want us to suffer the consequences of our sin when we don't heed the established boundaries or direction for our lives. But because we do sin, there often are unavoidable ramifications. God sets guidelines for living because He loves us. He seeks to bless and prosper us, but we must follow through in obedience to His Word.

As parents, it is not always joyful to punish and set boundaries with our teens. In fact, it is hard to have a tough love approach. But they will not learn obedience if we don't stick to what we need to do as parents. We may feel bad about doling out a punishment or taking privileges away. However, I would rather feel bad for that short moment of discomfort than to see my child in jail, overdosed, or dead because of my disobedience to God's wisdom and discipline. I shudder to think of the possibilities.

As for Daniela, she changed in several ways as a result of the rebellious road she traveled. It brought her back to the Lord in a way she had never experienced before. She saw God miraculously move in her life and came to understand God's love for her for the first time. The sentence for her crime included the threat of twenty years in prison, but was reduced to four months in juvie, followed by a program before returning home. And more—she heard her mom say, "Please forgive me for failing as a parent and not doing the right thing."

Have you allowed your teen to become embroiled in a dangerous situation due to a lack of tough love and the absence of consistently enforced boundaries? Know this—even if they are already in a dangerous place, you can ask God for mercy, forgiveness, and the grace to walk out His plan. God is waiting to receive you, hear you, and forgive you. His mercies are new every morning. He is faithful in every way. Repent sooner than later and seek God for His wisdom in all things.

It is never too late to do the God thing. The right thing. And God is never late to change you or your teen's circumstances.

If we confess our sins, he is faithful and just and will forgive us our sins and purify us from all unrighteousness.

1 John 1:9 NIV

Go Deeper

 What areas of your life as a parent have you not followed God's leading? Why?

 How can obedience to God's Word regarding your situation help your broken family?

 What do you need to do in order to repent and ask forgiveness for not being obedient and following through on what God had asked of you?

Meditate on Scripture

Keep this Book of the Law always on your lips; meditate on it day and night, so that you may be careful to do everything written in it. Then you will be prosperous and successful.

Joshua 1:8 NIV

This is what the Sovereign LORD, the Holy One of Israel, says: "In repentance and rest is your salvation, in quietness and trust is your strength, but you would have none of it."

Isaiah 30:15 NIV

Whoever conceals their sins does not prosper, but the one who confesses and renounces them finds mercy.

Proverbs 28:13 NIV

Pray

Dear Heavenly Father,

Words cannot express how much sorrow I feel for my disobedience towards You. I give my heart completely in repentance for my sins and for not following through as a parent and spouse. May Your Word stay on my lips and in my thoughts day and night. Help me to follow it to the best of my ability. Please Lord, extend mercy and grace towards me and my family. Guide me to follow the steps You have given in Your Word and to be obedient within my marriage so that trust can be built and relied on. When I am confronted with trouble, show me how to immediately go to You Lord and seek the answers instead of following after my own ways. Forgive my actions and sins and restore to wholeness.

Amen

SADNESS

I am worn out from groaning;
all night long I flood my bed with weeping
and drench my couch with tears.
Psalm 6:6 NIV

She sobbed in heart-wrenching lament as her head hit my lap. "Mom, just let me die. There's no place in this world for me. I don't want to live anymore, so just let me go to hell where I belong. I deserve it. Not even God could love me. I'm unlovable."

Abandoned as a baby with increased feelings of rejection, bullying throughout her young years by her own peers only added to her pain. She struggled to accept the Heavenly Father's love because she was too angry and hurt by others. Depression, self-hate, and brokenness drove her to cutting and a desire to harm others. She chose toxic friends and nearly died because of their dark influence on her. Yet, at the core of it all was an overwhelming hunger to be loved.

My heart ached with her. I felt the pain in her voice. Her wet tears flowed down my arms as I clasped her exhausted body. As she fell asleep and I pondered her pain.

The deep sadness in her soul poured over me. I sobbed, thinking of the words she'd just uttered, and whispered to God a prayer to heal Daniela's broken spirit. I asked God to do the same for me.

For days, I privately shed buckets of tears. I wept because I felt alone. I grieved because of her bad choices as well as the hurt I inflicted on her. I lamented the fact that she wasn't getting better. I mourned because as much as I wanted to be the one to take that shattered and bruised heart of hers and fix it, I knew it was impossible. Only God could heal her.

There is no way to describe the excruciating pain in my heart as a parent hearing my child cry out that she wants to die. Desolation took over her life, blinding her ability to see any future for herself. Suicidal thoughts preyed daily upon her mind. Medication overwhelmed her. She refused it, unable to handle even the lowest dose. I spent late nights driving from town to town with her in the car and the window down, playing Christian music to soothe her in the hopes that she might finally fall asleep.

But, God was watching over us. With counseling every week, our hearts lightened with a tiny smile here, and small laugh there. The tears remained, but in those moments of intense sadness, I imagined God gathering them all in His cupped hands. Each tear reflected the grief, the pain, the anguish, and the loss, collected like a sea of choppy waters, through which we both struggled to stay afloat and not be pulled under. That image of loving hands holding our tears and turbulence reminded me that we were not alone in this. God wept with us, too.

Soon her crushed spirit began to change. With continued prayer, her tears diminished. Prayer, with and for her, covered her with peace of mind. Sharing stories from the Bible and others in life who struggled just like us allowed her to dare to dream again. We both needed to know that we were not alone, and God saw our every tear.

As we persevered, hopelessness lifted. It didn't happen overnight. It took time. Lots of time.

Revelation 21:4 says that God will wipe away every tear from our eyes. Aren't you glad that He cares for us and feels our hurts and struggles as deeply as we do?

He cares for you and your family, too.

Today is the day to give Him all your tears. Let it all out. He hears you. He sees you. He wants to dry your tears once and for all.

Go Deeper

Some people see crying as a sign of weakness. In the Bible, there are many accounts of strong people of faith who cried out to the Lord and are not seen as weak. In fact, in 2 Corinthians 12:9 NIV it says: *But he said to me, "My grace is sufficient for you, for my power is made perfect in weakness." Therefore, I will boast all the more gladly about my weaknesses, so that Christ's power may rest on me.* Knowing this, do you believe God will be just as faithful to see you through your time of sadness?

Psalms 30:5 says weeping only lasts the night. That's right, our tears and sadness do not last forever. Joy does come. Read Ecclesiastes 3:4. How does this Scripture apply to you?

The Scripture in John 11:33, 35 NIV reads: *"When Jesus saw her weeping, and the Jews who had come along with her also weeping, he was deeply moved in spirit and troubled . . . Jesus wept."* What does this verse mean to you?

Meditate on Scripture

He will wipe every tear from their eyes. There will be no more death' or mourning or crying or pain, for the old order of things has passed away."

Revelation 21:4 NIV

For his anger lasts only a moment, but his favor lasts a lifetime; weeping may stay for the night but rejoicing comes in the morning.

Psalm 30:5 NIV

My face is red with weeping, dark shadows ring my eyes;

Job 16:16 NIV

You keep track of all my sorrows. You have collected all my tears in your bottle. You have recorded each one in your book.

Psalm 56:8 NLT

Pray

Dear Heavenly Father,

Oh, how I look forward to the day in heaven, when tears will be no more. This gives me great joy. I thank you Lord, that I have the ability to shed tears when I am hurting while on this earth. For every tear that comes, you collect and respond in love and compassion. To know that you can see and feel our broken hearts gives me comfort and hope. In response, You are moved to cry with me and my family. I know in faith that whenever I release myself in this way, I am allowing myself to also release those things upon my heart. I am so thankful that Your joy comes in the morning.

Amen

"Faith does not
eliminate questions.
But faith knows
where to take them."

— Elisabeth Elliot

SHAME

In you, LORD, I have taken refuge;
let me never be put to shame;
deliver me in your righteousness.
Psalm 31:1 NIV

Clad in black, long, pitch-black hair hung careless against her petite frame, as she walked quietly down the stairway. From the back, I first thought how pretty she looked in that stylish dress. Then she turned around.

Stitches. Doll-like, black marker stitches were scrawled across her face. Another one streaked across her neck and more traversed back and forth upon her arms and the front of her legs. In the guise of a Goth doll, she wanted to go to the mall with her father. He took one look at me and shook his head. He was not about to go anywhere with Daniela all dressed to go out in heavy makeup like that. He didn't call her Goth or Emo. He called her Gothmo.

Subculture idealism stood out in the forefront of Daniela's many identity issues. Goth and Emo played a big role in her life. Emo is linked to those who have major depression and hurts, with behaviors of suicidal ideology. Extreme in nature, they express their emotions using music, anime, and doll-like features displaying stitches to show that they are broken and need to be put back together again. Prone to impulsiveness, Emo's believe self-harm is a way to decrease the hurt and anguish they feel.

Those involved in the Goth culture idolize death, but not with suicidal thoughts. They like dark images, thoughts, and dramatic makeup. Goths lean toward cultic practices such as witchcraft. They also tend to be antisocial and sometimes introverted.

Because of those issues, we felt ashamed and embarrassed with Daniela's self-expression. Yes, we would tell her to take it off and she couldn't go to church looking like this. I sent Daniela to youth group with hopes of her hearing a message that might minister to her. She often returned with permanent marker words, drawings, or self-injury marks on her body from pins, paperclips, and anything that had a sharp point on it. This was something I could not control no matter how hard I tried. But somehow, others thought that I could.

In counseling, I learned cutting was one of the ways teens cope, helping them keep calm in anxious moments. This knowledge did not stop me from feeling humiliation. Since I valued privacy in the first place, I withdrew from everyone to keep judgmental comments from others at bay. The refuge of seclusion felt safe, though hiding made it more difficult to receive much needed ministry.

When I did voice some of my teen's issues aloud to

others, I felt a profound degree of failure as a parent. Not all friends and family understood. They did not know the many attempts to find help I had already initiated. I became frustrated and disgraced, certain I was secretly nominated for the "Worst Parent-of-the-Year Award."

In time, the Lord led me to healthy spiritual and psychological counsel. It was a pleasant surprise to hear that we were, in fact, doing a lot of good for our broken child when we guided her to adopt various means of self-expression in place of self-injury. My shame slowly dissipated.

Satan will do whatever is necessary using failure and condemnation to discourage parents. Yet, our biggest enemy is often ourselves. We sentence ourselves to a guilty verdict and allow the enemy to add heaps of unworthiness to our thoughts.

Christ's sacrificial death on the cross bore the affliction of all humanity's guilt and shame. He did not ask His heavenly Father to remove it. In fact, He took upon Himself every offense for the world to see. He didn't hide it. He didn't run from it. He faced it head on.

As parents of teens in crisis, we convince ourselves that we deserve shame, having brought our troubles upon ourselves. That is a lie. Jesus did not accept the lie. In fact, He took that lie and put it where it belonged—back on the very head of Satan. When Jesus suffered on the cross, His shed blood for our sin reminded Satan that we are precious, loved, forgiven, worthy, and redeemed. We have the victory in Him.

As one who once felt overwhelmed with shame, I can tell you this: Christ is bigger than shame and humiliation. Christ is also bigger than our adversary who seeks to shame us.

Today, Daniela uses her make-up creativity as a talented makeup artist. Our shame has become beauty for the eyes to behold. God is good.

Today, God wants you to live victoriously, even in the imperfection of your mistakes, failures, and sin. This in part, is how we mature and grow spiritually. Don't allow shame to encourage your belief that you are hopeless and beyond help. Don't withdraw yourself from others who can minister to you, shrinking back because you believed the shame lie. Take charge and make the choice to claim your freedom from shame by the blood of Jesus Christ.

Go Deeper

 Is there a particular area as a parent in which you feel shame? Write your thoughts on this exploring why it is there and what you can do about it.

 In Romans 8:1 it says that there is no condemnation for those in Christ Jesus. If shame condemns us, how can we be free from that kind of condemnation?

 How can we know that God's love for us on the cross is more than enough to cover the shame we may feel deep inside?

Meditate on Scripture

Because the Sovereign LORD helps me, I will not be disgraced. Therefore, have I set my face like flint, and I know I will not be put to shame.

Isaiah 50:7 NIV

As Scripture says, "Anyone who believes in him will never be put to shame."

Romans 10:11 NIV

Those who look to him are radiant; their faces are never covered with shame.

Psalm 34:5 NIV

Pray

Dear Heavenly Father,

Forgive me for allowing myself to remain in bondage with shame. I have let shame steal the peace You have for me in the midst of our situation and crises. Lord Jesus, You have taken my shame and nailed it on the cross once and for all. I know that I will not be disgraced again. As I stand in Your righteousness, guide me to recognize truth and to put shame where it belongs—under my feet. I know that anyone who believes in You will not be put to shame. When thoughts of shame come against me, I will believe and speak the name of Jesus to make those words null and void. By doing so, shame will be defeated.

Amen

"But God doesn't call us to be comfortable. He calls us to trust Him so completely that we are unafraid to put ourselves in situations where we will be in trouble if He doesn't come through."

— Francis Chan

SHOCK

I keep my eyes always on the LORD.
With him at my right hand, I will not be shaken.
Psalm 16:8 NIV

Crisis assaults you. You're numb. In utter shock. Like walking out of the water on the beach when an unexpected whammy of a wave cuts you across the back. You didn't see it coming.

Once it slaps you, the true nature of the impact penetrates your being. Automatically, your mind races, seeking the best response for protection. A buffer wake-up-wall surrounds you, warding off a storm of emotions that could take you under the water completely. Such sudden crises are little zaps of emotional surprise that leave our heads shaking in wonder once we drag ourselves onto dry sand.

Then there are the giant shockwaves that take us to another place outside of reality, like another planet. I have been jolted both ways multiple times. I know what it is to be paralyzed in my mind, completely shut down. I didn't know how to respond. Life continued around me, but I remained chained in a dead zone. I felt like a robot, mechanically getting by on commands I was programmed to do.

"Well Stacy," you may ask, "what kind of shocking things have you had to deal with?"

"How have I been shocked?" I respond in my best Shakespearean sonnet voice, "Let me count the ways . . ."

- How about the time I blinked in astonishment when my daughter told me she didn't want to be a girl. She thought it was unfair of God to not allow her to make the decision on her own of what gender she should be. She was serious.

- In her preteen years, she astounded me with a list of friends she spent hours with on social media—all fabricated by her—because the friends she had in real life hurt her over and over again.

- And dumbfounded was I the day I found her in the bathroom trying to bleach her skin because she hated the color she was born with. She spent weeks and weeks scouring the internet for different products to make her appear lighter, lamenting how she looked in her own skin.

- Then there was the time I walked in on her to find her stomach sliced up from a razor. She said cutting on the outside was actually less painful than the hurt she felt inside. I told her that she could accidentally kill herself, to which she replied, "Death doesn't hurt you. Life does."

As she aged, some of Daniela's abandonment and rejection issues that stemmed from being adopted grew larger. I did not understand the severity of the problems she carried until she dropped a shock-bomb during a counseling session.

In that session, I learned she had connected to a thirteen-year-old male through a cartoon fantasy-world game online with parental controls. Somehow, this site took her out of the game and into a video chat room. He befriended her for a year and was the only kid she felt a kinship with because he supposedly shared the same abandonment and rejection woes.

After a year, he threatened to kill her and our family if she did not strip down naked in the video. This was the beginning of her PTSD. It worsened when she saw two teens over the internet commit suicide. Feeling at fault for what they did, she assumed the role of rescuer within these toxic relationships.

I was stunned.

Things began to make sense. I thought I had protected her by locking my laptop, having serious discussions with her, and taking things away when boundaries were crossed. But none of these safeguards protected her. Somehow, the enemy still slithered into her world, leading to a more depressed child. The impact of this revelation left me speechless and disturbed. Shocked beyond reason.

To think about food, communicate with others, or make basic decisions was impossible. I did not have the energy to move or think. Dazed and numb to do even the smallest task, I couldn't cook or even dress myself. Such things required too much effort.

The residue of the shockwaves—like the destructive aftershocks of earthquakes—held me captive for days. As weeks passed, the shock dulled, yet the numbness persisted. Time seems to stand still when you've dealt with so much heartache and loss.

Through it all, my love for God never wavered. My faith faced many challenges. Sometimes it soared high and other times it plummeted low. Despite all of the reckless and rebellious decisions my daughter made because of her pain, I knew that the Lord loved her and had never left either of us. God was right there with us—with her—in the moment of need. I could not stop what was transpiring in Daniela's life, but I could stop and ask God to intervene where I could not.

In some aspect, the shock that took place after each ordeal was a safety net to sustain me from going into a severe depression. Each shock compelled me to draw closer to God. In that place, He used shock to shield and comfort us. As we go to the Lord for help, He peels back the layers of shock and awe to show us the things we need to learn in order to guide our child, as well as us, into healing.

Go Deeper

When in shock, we are often bewildered, perplexed, and dazed. These kinds of events can leave the strongest person in the world feeling weak and helpless. The fact is, God in His omniscience, already knew about that shocking thing. He is never shocked. Knowing this, how can we find help from our Heavenly Father when we are in the midst of shock?

Shock can bring about many side effects such as physical sickness, inability to focus, and rollercoaster moods. Outbursts of anger or uncontrollable crying are normal, too. How do you react when you come across a situation that leaves you in a state of shock? How can God help you through it?

Meditate on Scripture

But whoever listens to me will dwell secure and will be at ease, without dread of disaster.

Proverbs 1:33 ESV

But this I call to mind, and therefore I have hope: The steadfast love of the Lord never ceases; his mercies never come to an end; they are new every morning; great is your faithfulness.

Lamentations 3:21-23 ESV

Pray

Dear Heavenly Father,

Nothing happens without Your knowledge or permission. No matter what shocks me, You are never surprised. You shelter me with Your wings and wrap Your arms of love around me when I am fearful. Help me to listen and remember that You are my anchor and I can stand secure in the rocky, shocking, reckless seas of life. I can be at peace without worry or dread because You uphold me with Your right hand. Your steadfast love never ceases, and Your mercies never come to an end. I am so thankful they are new every morning for great is Your faithfulness in my time of need.

Amen

STRESS

For our struggle is not against flesh and blood,
but against the rulers, against the authorities,
against the powers of this dark world and against the
spiritual forces of evil in the heavenly realms.
Ephesians 6:12 NIV

Standing in the hotel lobby before the welcome desk, I couldn't wait to sign my name and get the key to my room. With my overnight bag in hand, I stepped into the elevator. Pressing the shiny red button for the doors to close, I let out a huge sigh of exhaustion. Stress had worn me to a frazzle.

I felt torn as I numbly pushed open the heavy door to my room. Should I have left the house to keep my mental state intact? Or, should I have stayed to keep my child from falling apart? The questions repeated over and over in my head. *How much more can I endure, God?*

I sighed. In defeat, guilt washed over me like a flood of icy water, fully enveloping me as punishment for trying to escape my stress fractured home and every familiar thing I held dear.

I was in crisis. Retreat seemed my only option.

Attacks from every quarter buffeted me in the days prior to this moment until I hit a breaking point. Assaulted from every side, my head spun in confusion:

- A letter from a woman at church criticized my parenting.
- An email from another person chastised me for the actions of my daughter.
- The never-ending drama of my daughter's self-esteem and rejection issues, anger, cutting, anxiety, and so much more, closed in on me.

My supportive husband promised to hold down the fort while I took a much-needed break. However, my lost and broken, out-of-control teenager saw my need to get away for a rest very differently. It served to only heightened the abandonment issues she'd wrestled with since birth.

Leaving my normal routine did not diminish my stress level. It only intensified. I fell to my knees begging for help from God and anyone who would listen. Thankfully, in this place of retreat and escape, the Lord met me with an answer to my cries. I opened my treasured Bible, worn from use, asking God to show me what to do. Scripture after Scripture leapt off the page as He reminded me of the many stressful situations His followers endured and His sure promises for provision and rescue in the midst of them.

I was reminded of Joshua, left with the huge responsibility to bring the people of Israel into the Promised Land after Moses died. Then there was the Apostle Paul, beaten and left for dead because he preached the Gospel. In their time of desperation, they cried out to their Heavenly Father. They did not run off to a hotel thinking they'd get away from their problems like I had.

They drew near to God, and He drew near to them.

For too long my pride got in the way of finding resolution to my problems. I thought I could handle everything myself. In my own power. Errors in judgment made things worse. What a mess! Everything, including myself, spun out of control.

But in that moment of retreat, drawing nearer to my God in a whirlpool of unrelenting stress, I sat on that hotel bed literally hugging my Bible as a safety net in my storm. God was my anchor, holding me in place so I wouldn't be drowned under the wild current. My only hope was the belief that God could do for me what He did for Joshua and Paul.

Our struggles are not just emotional, mental, or physical. They are also spiritual. In fact, Ephesians 6:12 says that we are daily at war with ourselves as well as our teens and young adults. It is a war against the forces of evil as we fight to save our sanity and our children's lives.

I thought running away for a respite would solve

229

my problems, but they came along with me like a packed suitcase, like heavy baggage that would not allow me to rest. My selfish reaction to run away only exacerbated the open wounds of all my volatile and complicated issues. This led to a sleepless night in a strange place, and a teen feeling abandoned back home.

Only when I dropped before God under the weight of it, did my heart and mind find a hope and solution in the midst of my turmoil. Yes, I needed rest. We all do. In fact, it's biblical. It is important and necessary for parents to find a restful place to regroup and be strengthened during an emotional crisis within the home. This was to be the emphasis of my retreat from the front lines. I didn't need to run away to fill myself with happy distractions. I needed to run to God to be renewed with the wings of eagles.

God wants us to enter into His peace and rest and look to Him in our difficult circumstances. When we try to find it on our own, stress grips us in a fierce stronghold. How do we find the rest that comes from God while in the middle of a crisis?

- Bathe yourself in prayer, even if you only have the strength to say, "Jesus."
- Ask those who will keep your confidence to intercede for you.
- Surround yourself with the Word. Read, pray, and insert your name and the name of your children into the Scriptures.
- Find support through books and websites. The

Resources section at the end of this book gives more information about this.

- Listen to music that lifts your spirit and ministers encouragement and peace to your heart.
- Seek therapy through referrals from friends, church, and support groups. There are many who offer great wisdom and counsel. Ask and trust God to lead you to the right person.

Fighting a battle by yourself can leave you stressed and alone. This is exactly what the enemy of our soul wants. You are not just fighting this battle through the flesh but also in the spirit. Therefore, you need to be spiritually prepared with God leading the charge. Dealing with a teen in crisis is stressful. Let us run to our victorious warrior, Jesus Christ, to fight our battles for us as we rest in Him.

Go Deeper

 What are some ways that you can run to God in the midst of a crisis?

 List five things you can do to help alleviate your stress. Then ask God to provide a way to those things as an answer to prayer.

Psalm 18:6 NASB says, *"In my distress I called upon the Lord, and cried to my God for help; He heard my voice out of His temple, and my cry for help before Him came into His ears."* The next time you feel stressed, how will you apply this Scripture?

Meditate on Scripture

And the peace of God, which surpasses all comprehension, will guard your hearts and your minds in Christ Jesus.

Philippians 4:7 NASB

In my distress I prayed to the LORD, and the LORD answered me and set me free.

Psalm 118:5 NLT

Come to me, all you who are weary and burdened, and I will give you rest.

Matthew 11:28 NIV

Pray

Dear Heavenly Father,

My flesh and my heart may fail, but You, O God, are the strength of my heart and my portion forever. Yes, I am weary and burdened but You give me rest. I will cast all my anxieties upon You, because You care for me. Help me to be anxious for nothing, but to come to You in prayer and supplication. With thanksgiving, let my requests be made known to you O God. May Your peace, which passes all understanding, guard my heart and my mind in You, Christ Jesus. Yes, let my soul find rest in You my God; for my hope comes from You.

Amen

UNFORGIVENESS

And whenever you stand praying,
forgive, if you have anything against anyone,
so that your Father also who is in heaven
may forgive you your trespasses.
Mark 11:25 ESV

"I want my life back!" I silently raged within. *"I'm tired of trying to rescue you, defend you, deal with every problem in the book because of your rebelliousness, selfishness, destructive behaviors, and not caring about yourself or what you are putting me through."*

Under my breath the words spilled in a spitting fit of anger. I seethed from the sense of feeling like a doormat to be walked upon—stomped upon—expected to love my daughter even though she treated me in such a fashion, purposely or not. I knew she wrestled with serious issues such as PTSD, major anxiety, mood disorder, and self-harm, to name a few. But at the same time, I did teach her right from wrong. She should know better.

The disturbing drama played out time and again. How many times did I show forgiveness? Too many to count. It wearied me. Why was I the one doing all the forgiving? She's the one who put me through such agonies that I didn't know if I was coming or going—or who I was as a person anymore. I lost myself in her turbulent world, a slave to its chaos. It impeded my ability to make rational parental decisions, or act like a reasonable adult among my own peers.

Pain. Oh, what pain Daniela caused me! Her actions troubled me deeply. When moments of forgiveness were sought by her after an episode, I forgave her. But secretly, I grew resentful every day.

Bitterness developed in my heart. Shame and Embarrassment resided there too. They anchored into the foundation of my being, bricks of unforgiveness slowly building a wall between me and my daughter. Between me and my God. I did not detest or despise my daughter. I did in fact love her tremendously. But escalating battles and constant distress in various forms stirred anger and misery in my soul and spirit.

I behaved in a short-tempered manner towards others. My self-esteem as a parent dwindled. I enjoyed precious little time to think about myself and my needs. Her actions depleted us financially as we tried to secure counsel and help for her. Our lifestyle of constant crises caused me to withdraw from friends and fellowship. Why couldn't I have a normal life like everyone else? I sighed in exasperation at my life spinning out of control.

This sowed into my heart and spirit a prolonged negativity and a swell of unforgiveness. Grace and Mercy abandoned me. My emotional state hardened around a hatred for the constant upheaval of burdens my daughter shoveled and dumped on my shoulders to carry. To show forgiveness felt like enabling her with a free pass to continue in this abusive pattern. How could I really forgive such painful offences?

I knew in my heart I must forgive as an obedient child of God. He first forgave me. The Lord clearly states the forgiveness mandate in Ephesians 4:31-32 NIV: *"Get rid of all bitterness, rage and anger, brawling and slander, along with every form of malice. Be kind and compassionate to one another, forgiving each other, just as in Christ God forgave you."*

God's call to minister the medicine of forgiveness is a hard pill to swallow when fury burned within every fiber of my being. To not forgive imprisoned me in a cycle of bondage. In desperation, at the end of my rope, as I turned to God—my only hope—I realized I needed to make a choice: Stay enslaved to a spirit of unforgiveness or learn to truly forgive. The God-kind of forgiveness.

In one revelatory moment, I understood how I never mourned the losses in my life. Harboring unforgiveness overshadowed them. So, I stopped to grieve over lost time missing out on fun times with my friends and relaxing with hobbies I loved to do. I ached over the financial depletion of our savings trying to rescue our daughter over and over.

I groaned in sorrow over the details of my daughter's countless crises that put me on an emotional roller coaster. I lamented the loss of many days and nights spent in tears that might not have been if Daniela didn't have these issues. This was not the life journey I chose to travel. I mourned not having the perfect family that I wanted.

But, how was I to move on to forgiveness knowing there would be another crisis on the horizon?

The answer came in an unexpected moment through a conversation with my daughter. I openly said that I was sorry for all of the mistakes I made as a parent. She candidly responded to my openness, "Mom, you are a great parent. I'm the one to blame. I knew what was right and what was wrong, but I was angry at the world, my relationships, and at God for many reasons. You were only trying to help me in the best way you thought. In the end, it was still my choice, my decision, my life. Even if it was all wrong."

In that precious moment, God revealed the error of her ways to her. Sometimes our children do not acknowledge their fault. They don't know how. However, when we do our part and model forgiveness, steeped in prayer and dependence on God, they one day come to a realization about their own accountability before God.

Forgiveness empowers us to bring healing into hurtful situations when we lovingly express the pain felt by the actions of others against us. We choose to make amends as the Bible instructs in Colossians 3:12 NIV: *"Bear with each other and forgive one another if any of you has a grievance against someone. Forgive as the Lord forgave you."*

God's work to cleanse our hearts, clears away the obstacles of bitterness and anger so we are free to truly forgive others—even those closest to us who hurt us the most. Even others, like friends and relatives, who may have stepped upon our hearts with careless or judgmental words or actions.

Unforgiveness will rear its ugly head once in a while, when another offense, cutting comment, or distressing crisis comes along. But I promise you this: When forgiveness flows freely, the wellspring of unforgiveness recedes and joy streams in, filling every crevice of your heart.

For some, extending forgiveness takes time and prayer to prepare the soul to obey the will of the Spirit. For others, it's a matter of obedience to follow through on God's direction.

However you find your path to forgiveness, peace of mind and hope in heart await you there.

Go Deeper

 Are there roots of unforgiveness in your heart that you have been holding on to? If so, name them?

D.L. Moody said: "The voice of sin is loud, but the voice of forgiveness is louder." How does this apply to you?

Assignment: Write down the pain, hurts, and losses you have mourned or are mourning now, and ask God to restore and heal you. Write down the offenses your daughter/son have done against you and ask God to help you forgive them one by one the way He has done for you. Then pray and thank God for His forgiveness as He refreshes you with a new attitude of forgiveness towards your child.

Action: If someone has caused hurt in the past in which you struggle to forgive in the present, then consider counsel for that pain. Oftentimes we need our mental, emotional, and physical bodies to heal first before opening our heart to the spiritual aspects of forgiveness. You will know when it is the right time to add forgiveness to your healing arsenal. Seek God. He will quietly minister to you in His own way to show you when and how to walk in it.

Meditate on Scripture

Make every effort to live in peace with everyone and to be holy; without holiness no one will see the Lord.

Hebrews 12:14 NIV

Put on then, as God's chosen ones, holy and beloved, compassionate hearts, kindness, humility, meekness, and patience, bearing with one another and, if one has a complaint against another, forgiving each other; as the Lord has forgiven you, so you also must forgive.

Colossians 3:12-13 ESV

But one whom you forgive anything, I forgive also; for indeed what I have forgiven, if I have forgiven anything, I did it for your sakes in the presence of Christ, so that no advantage would be taken of us by Satan, for we are not ignorant of his schemes.

2 Corinthians 2:10-11 NIV

Pray

Dear Heavenly Father,

Help me make every effort to live in peace as much as it depends on me and to strive to live in holiness. If I have seeds of unforgiveness, please reveal them to me Lord. Let forgiveness rule my heart and emotions in times when a negative word or situation with my child comes my way. May my response be filled with loving-kindness that pleases You and not one of anger or bitterness that pleases the enemy. Show me how to extend forgiveness in the same manner as You have given towards me. May I exude humility, meekness, patience, compassion, and forgiveness, the way You have shown me. Guide my thoughts towards grace and mercy just as You have with my child, so that I can be an example of Christ's love.

Amen

"I've read the last page
of the Bible.
It's all going to turn out
all right."

— Billy Graham

UNREST

You will keep in perfect peace those whose minds are
steadfast, because they trust in you.
Isaiah 26:3 NIV

I live in a perpetual state of unrest. I wake every morning conscious of an underlying agitation deep within me. It's not supposed to be this way, but when you have a kid in crisis, unrest is your daily companion. It takes a toll upon your mental, physical, emotional, and spiritual well-being.

How about you? Do you feel the roar of cyclone winds reverberating through your being from the inside out? All. The. Time?

Sometimes, when I feel that an issue resolved itself, and a settled calm envelops me, gross reality slaps me like an unexpected wave, stinging me with salt and smart. It turns out to be another eye of the storm deception. Before I know it, the back winds whip up again and I shake in upheaval, uncertainty, and unrest. Hurricane force winds spawn random tornados. I can't seem to steady myself in the disturbance.

241

I define unrest as the constant state of disruption, trouble, emotional turbulence, strife, and every other word descriptive of the opposite of peace. It's like a ceaseless "disturbance in the Force"; a never-ending light-saber duel between Luke Skywalker and Darth Vader. This battle takes place in my mind with an unrelenting assault of confusion, frustration, and discouragement.

Some of these moments manifest in a barrage of tormenting thoughts: What if I make the wrong choice for a treatment program or counselor? Would this cause more chaos and rebellion? What if I help my daughter in a particular area of her life that is not following God's lead, but my own? What if I made the correct decision of what God wanted me to do but was too fearful to act on it?

Where can peace be found in the midst of such turmoil and unrest?

Job 3:26 NIV says, *"I have no peace, no quietness; I have no rest, but only turmoil."* Stripped of every comfort in a season of testing, Job endured a depth of unrest that many parents of teens in crisis can identify with in one way or another. His trial was unrelenting until he laid himself fully upon the mercy of the Lord.

But Job wasn't the only character in the Bible who struggled with unrest. Queen Esther faced fierce winds of unrest, too, requiring her to take a risk in order to surmount her inner turmoil. Under the storm clouds of impending genocide, Esther was challenged to take action and save the

Jewish people from the murderous plans of Haman, King Xerxes's right-hand man.

Haman hated the Jews. He made it his goal to seek revenge against them for a perceived humiliation at their hands.

Being in a unique and empowered position within the palace, young and inexperienced Queen Esther made a brave decision. Pacing back and forth within the grandiose palace walls, she must have agonized over what to do. Tossed about on billowing waves of confusion and unrest, she realized that she, alone, stood in the gap between Israel and their annihilation. The choice of life or death was before her.

Treading the rough waves, how did Esther rise above the waters of unrest and find solid ground to land upon where the wind and waves ceased? She fasted. She prayed. She cried out to God for deliverance—and called others to do the same.

God gave Queen Esther the courage necessary to execute a clever plan and boldly confront both her people's accuser and the king who could calm the death threats of a churning sea. Following through on the Lord's leading, Esther became God's instrument of deliverance for Israel, and punishment for wicked Haman. Her example of seeking God's face and help, while being willing to do as He commanded, no matter how fearsome a feat required, illustrates a powerful principle. Parents battling the inner turmoil of unrest due to unresolved issues in the life of their troubled teen are wise to follow her example in their times of crisis and tough life choices.

Be an Esther today. God guided her and strengthened her. He will do the same for you. Break the chains of unrest through fasting and prayer. Cry out to the Lord for His mercy in total brokenness. Remain steadfast in His Word. Pray continually. Trust in your Heavenly Father in Whom you have placed your faith.

There, God will anchor you. There, you will find peace from your unrest.

Go Deeper

 How can you turn your restless days and nights around so that you can live in peace and contentment in Christ?

 What other Bible men and women displayed unrest in their situations? How did they find peace and contentment in the midst of unrest?

 Esther's dire circumstances pushed her to pray and fast until God delivered her. What do you need to do for your teen and family to be delivered?

Note: Fasting is important in breaking the strongholds that bind us and our family. But, not everyone can physically fast food due to health issues. There are many different ways of fasting such as choosing one food item and abstaining from it, not watching television, or limiting social media activity. Ask the Lord to reveal how and what to fast from and use that time to seek the Him.

Meditate on Scripture

This is what the LORD says: "Stand at the crossroads and look; ask for the ancient paths, ask where the good way is, and walk in it, and you will find rest for your souls . . ."

Jeremiah 6:16 NIV

Truly my soul finds rest in God; my salvation comes from him.

Psalm 62:1 NIV

For God is not a God of disorder but of peace—as in all the congregations of the Lord's people.

1 Corinthians 14:33 NIV

Pray

Dear Heavenly Father,

Unrest in my heart does not help my daughter or my family. It only drives me away from You. Heavenly Father, help me to recognize that unrest does not come from You but from Satan, the perpetrator of our unrest and thief of our peace. Show me how to be more like Queen Esther. When I stand at the crossroads and am not sure where to go, show me God's way and help me walk in it.

Remind me that the only way to break through unrest in my heart is by seeking You. Truly, my soul will find rest in You for my salvation comes from You. Thank you, Lord, that You are not a God of disorder, but one of order. Of peace. Heavenly Father, I will pray Your Word and fast according to what You have asked of me. May my sight be focused on You and not on my circumstances so that unrest dissolves into peace.

Amen

VULNERABILITY

Then as I looked over the situation, I called together the
nobles and the rest of the people and said to them, "Don't
be afraid of the enemy! Remember the Lord, who is great
and glorious, and fight for your brothers, your sons, your
daughters, your wives, and your homes!"
Nehemiah 4:14 NLT

I was ecstatic. After browsing the internet for days in
search of a house to rent, I finally found a home within our
family budget and contacted the owner to see if it was still
available.

Studying all the pictures on the site, I read every
tempting detail about wood floors, new appliances, the
back patio, and more. I fell in love with the place. The
owner swiftly replied to my email and confirmed, "Yes, it
is still available." He clarified his picky position as to the
type of people he wanted as renters and prioritized that the
property be kept intact, clean, and well cared for.

The next message I received from him touched my
heart with the inclusion of a Scripture verse at the end. This
is so God, I thought. Soon, the email arrived announcing
that our family was chosen from a number of applicants as

the new renters to occupy his beautiful home. An attached lease was ready for our review.

Our exhilaration rose like a kite, bouncing joyfully on a happy wind current. But all too soon a gust of violent reality swept the euphoria in securing our dream house out of reach. We were the victims of a scam. The scam artist, presenting himself as the owner of a house for rent, preyed on the weak with a tantalizing bait. He even went so far as to use God's Word to entice and deceive anyone vulnerable enough to pass his way. I became just another vulnerable prey to the trap.

But that's not surprising. Being a parent of a teen in crisis for many years, vulnerability comes with the territory.

Like our high hopes when we thought we'd secured our dream house, only to be bitterly disappointed, we'd get our hopes up when it seemed our daughter had turned a leaf and learned some valuable lessons. We'd make plans for her future. We'd reach out to others to work with her as guides and mentors.

But this hopeful spirit didn't last. The ceiling swiftly fell in on our enthusiasm which left us discouraged, physically and mentally weak, and looking to God to understand what happened. We wanted to give up, captive to our circumstances.

Our weak vulnerability made us susceptible to finding ways to cope with our emotional guilt and pain. For me, not eating became normal. For my husband, a glass of wine grew beyond a simple glass to cope and spiraled out of control. His stress levels exploded to new highs and opened the door to several strokes. Our vulnerabilities in a time of crisis swelled into binding chains.

I wondered if I would ever be set free from the burdens that bruised our spirits. Somewhere along the timeline of crises, our protective foundations cracked and crumbled from the damage. Similar to the city of Jerusalem in the Book of Nehemiah, we were left unprotected and vulnerable by a barrage of attacks from the enemy.

Nehemiah saw the powerlessness of Israel in the wake of their captivity. He heard about the assaults upon them, leaving them defenseless within the broken walls of Jerusalem. He presented a plan before God, a plan to rebuild the walls and empower the people to protect themselves so they would no longer be vulnerable to the enemy.

The only way to rebuild our family's foundation was to break the spiritual strongholds which exposed our family to attacks. Our spiritual life was like the cracked and crumbled walls of Jerusalem, broken for so long. To rebuild and restore required many changes:

Church Home

One of the first changes we made was the foundation stone of a new church home. As much as we loved many of the people from our old church, we needed to start anew and leave behind the painful incidences and memories we experienced there. My husband sought a personal, spiritual revival and gained a fresh perspective in the Word of God. I worked through severe depression and surrounded myself with people who did not know of our struggles and personal problems allowing for a fresh start in new relationships. Walking away from forty years of ministry, worship, and fellowship was a difficult decision to make. Through this time of heightened vulnerability, God drew near to us on our journey into the unknown and gave us peace.

Confession

Our next course of action in rebuilding the foundation for our family involved the confession of our faults and crying out in brokenness to God over our losses. By confession, we admitted our mistakes, sin, and liabilities as parents. Confession is hard because it opens us to conviction and correction—not always a pleasant thing—but vital. Confession kicks pride from our doorstep so it can no longer block our family from opening the door of restoration we so desperately needed.

Strategy

To reconstruct our lives, we asked the Lord to show us a specific strategy. We could not rely on what we thought was best. Been there. Done that. Failed at every corner turned in our own wisdom. We learned the hard way how God's paths are clearer when we fully open ourselves to be guided by Him.

Vigilance

Be brave and strong. Remember, whatever God

rebuilds, Satan will oppose—as Nehemiah learned while rebuilding Jerusalem. He remained vigilant, on constant alert. Israel's enemies taunted him daily as he sought to obey God's directions in rebuilding the walls of Jerusalem. But God's strength and courage empowered him. So too, God's power to defeat your enemies' taunts are sufficient.

Prayer

Cover every foundation stone in your family's life with intercessory prayer to expose areas of vulnerability. The enemy loves to creep in through tiny crevices and cause havoc. Leave nothing open, not even a crack. Do not allow Satan to get a foothold into your home.

Support

Find support along your journey—a vital prescription for the healing process. My husband connected with an excellent addiction recovery group made up of fellow Christians where he was free to share his heartache as a parent and leave his guilt behind. Journaling became my outlet. Writing letters to God, sharing on my blog, and opening up with very close friends who understood the grief and despair of a broken parent comforted me in time of need.

Scripture

Lastly, secure your family's foundations in the Word of God. This builds your walls strong and thick where even the smallest weapon cannot penetrate or bring destruction. Put on the armor of God daily through immersion in Bible reading and memorization.

Go Deeper

 Read Nehemiah 4. The workers rebuilding the walls were ridiculed, discouraged, and attacked-- much like parents with teens in crisis are forced to endure. However, Nehemiah encouraged them as recorded in verses fourteen and fifteen. How can you apply those verses to your crisis?

Building and/or restoring a firm foundation for your home life is important to maintain health and administer healing for your broken family. What are three elements discussed in this chapter that make your family's foundations solid?

What must you personally do to keep your family from being vulnerable?

Meditate on Scripture

For no one can lay any foundation other than the one already laid, which is Jesus Christ.

1 Corinthians 3:11 NIV

Put on the full armor of God, so that you can take your stand against the devil's schemes.

Ephesians 6:11 NIV

Be strong and courageous. Do not be afraid or terrified because of them, for the Lord your God goes with you; he will never leave you nor forsake you.

Deuteronomy 31:6 NIV

Unless the LORD builds the house, they labor in vain who build it; Unless the LORD guards the city, the watchman keeps awake in vain.

Psalm 127:1 NASB

Pray

Dear Heavenly Father,

Your Word tells us to build a strong foundation in You. By doing so, we will be able to block the enemy's attacks on our family. We can do this by preparing our hearts spiritually to hear Your voice through Your Word and praying at all times against the devil's schemes. Show us how to keep areas of our lives fortified from vulnerability to attack. May we be strong and courageous, not afraid or terrified, because You go before us and will not leave or forsake us. Father, You are the foundation I want to build our house upon. If we build it on our own understanding and strengths, we build it in vain and it will fail. Give us wisdom and protection from cracks of vulnerability in every foundation stone of our lives.

Amen

"Sometimes you must
stand still
in order to get moving
to where God
wants you to go."

— D.A. McBride

WEARY

He gives strength to the weary and increases
the power of the weak.
Isaiah 40:29 NIV

Standing over the kitchen sink, I cried buckets of tears over the dirty dishes. *"How much more can I take, Lord? I'm tired. Too tired to pray. Too tired to think. Too tired to keep moving."*

Rest. Oh, how I needed rest.

I'm not talking about physical rest alone. I knew I needed spiritual, emotional, and mental rest. The avalanche of Daniela's problems wearied me. Barraged on a daily basis with crisis after crisis, I was worn thin as paper and sleep deprived like a zombie. Oh, how I wanted to snooze away my problems like a hibernating bear in winter.

Tired and exhausted, I looked for every opportunity to hide from my teen. I craved just fifteen minutes of solace. Surely, that was not asking too much, was it? Moments stolen to gaze mindlessly out the window, watch birds flit about, or peacefully listen to the wind provided a small haven of enjoyment. Sneaking aside for such an instant now and then, gave me a sense of peaceful strength.

But most of the time, those minutes of relief were overshadowed by grim reality. My mind constantly raced, set on perpetual emergency alert. Would I need to take my daughter to the hospital after a self-injury? Would I have to jump in my car at the last second and chase after her as she ran out and slammed the door? Would tonight be another night to stay awake, standing guard in the darkness until she came out of another depressive episode? These thoughts sapped my life energy, depleting my inner strength like water swirling down the drain.

Spiritually, I felt dead. As much as I tried, I could not gather the words to pray. In such empty moments, I relied on Romans 8:26 NIV: *"In the same way, the Spirit helps us in our weakness. We do not know what we ought to pray for, but the Spirit himself intercedes for us through wordless groans."* For a long time, those words were the only anchor I clung to through the turbulent storms I faced.

Most days I cried out to God in a mere whisper under my breath, seeking comfort and encouragement in the midst of my exhaustion. Jesus knew and understood the emotional and physical burnout I wrestled with. The Holy Spirit remained faithful in bringing Scriptures to my mind, providing me a blessed assurance and fuel to keep going.

Adapting pertinent Scriptures as prayers, I felt empowered with hope. But other times, overwhelmed in weariness, the only prayers I could murmur were, "Jesus" and "Holy Spirit help me." Those prayers work too.

Upon reflection of such weary days, it amazes me how God's presence settled over me in the midst of my weakness. He gave me the strength I needed to get through each day. I couldn't always see it then due to the ferocity of how circumstances engulfed me, but eventually I learned to keep my eyes upon Him rather than my crisis. Because He is faithful, His eyes remained steadfast upon me.

His eyes remain steadfast upon you, too.

Although God meets us in our seasons of weariness, it's important to make sensible efforts to care for ourselves. Eating well, finding time and encouragement with a devoted friend, and taking restful naps are just a few things that provide benefits to wellbeing. In addition, I also found walking to be restful, writing out my thoughts and feelings in a God journal, and doing something that I enjoyed like watching a movie with popcorn under the covers of my bed. Although I could not indulge in all of these things as a daily routine, I incorporated them into my lifestyle as special getaways to cherish.

Meditating on God's Word keeps my mind renewed and at peace as well as listening to music to calm my soul. This is how God pours His spirit of refreshing and renewal over and within us.

The more you purpose to lean into Christ, the more

you are strengthened by Him. God never intended for you to carry such a heavy load. Not only can He can lift your burdens, He can carry you, too. You only need to ask and He who is faithful will do it.

Go Deeper

 There are times when weariness settles upon us with a capital "W." List three ways to find rest for your mental, physical, and spiritual health.

Romans 8:26 explains how the Holy Spirit speaks for us when we have no words. How does this comfort you as a parent when you feel you have nothing left to give?

Your Heavenly Father provides a Comforter for you through your trials. Read 2 Corinthians 12:9-10. Use this Scripture to write about how can you change your weakness into strength?

Meditate on Scripture

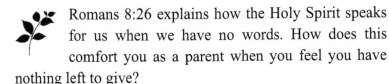

Blessed be the God and Father of our Lord Jesus Christ, the Father of mercies and God of all comfort, who comforts us in all our affliction so that we will be able to comfort those who are in any affliction with the comfort with which we ourselves are comforted by God. For just as the sufferings of Christ are ours in abundance, so also our comfort is abundant through Christ.

2 Corinthians 1:3-5 NASB

God is our refuge and strength, an ever-present help in trouble.

Psalm 46:1 NIV

But you, LORD, do not be far from me. You are my strength; come quickly to help me.

Psalm 22:19 NIV

Pray

Dear Heavenly Father,

Thank You for Your comfort when I am weak and afflicted. I pray that the comfort You give to me, I am able to give to others when they need to be comforted. Jesus, I long to dwell in Your presence and find my refuge, strength, and ever-present help in time of trouble. Provide me the durability and energy I need to get through each day. Lead me to find rest in Your Word and in my time of worship with You. When burdens weary and overwhelm me, You are my portion of grace and comfort. Remind me that You are ever so near and will lift me up when I think I cannot go on any longer. Renew and refresh my mind, as well as strengthen my spirit.

Amen

"Worry does not empty
tomorrow of its sorrows;
it empties today
of its strength."

— Corrie Ten Boom

WORRY

Peace I leave with you; my peace I give you. I do not give to you as the world gives. Do not let your hearts be troubled and do not be afraid.
John 14:27 NIV

On July 9, 1958, in Lituya Bay, Alaska, an earthquake shook the ground under the Fairweather Fault creating a massive rock fall from about 3000 feet high, dropping into the waters of the Giblet Inlet. *Geoscience News and Information* at Geology.com claims that this set off a 1,720-foot-high mega tsunami so strong, it leveled millions of trees and vegetation from the inlet, across land, and into the Gulf of Alaska.

Who would have thought that a tremor so deep in the ground could cause such massive turbulence and destruction above?

Earthquakes are easily compared to the emotional state of worry. The constant worries over our hurting or rebellious child are like accumulated tremors over time that take their toll with no release. When emotional tremors build up deep inside our hearts and minds, the turbulence eventually bursts, crashing over the landscape of our lives with such fury that it carves a path of monumental suffering and pain in its wake.

For me, these eruptions caused a breakdown in my very core with exhaustion and irrepressible tears to the point of gasping for air, depressive and suicidal thoughts, and a mountain of worry I could not control. I couldn't leave my room or deal with my daughter. And of all things, I become tele-phobic. I didn't even know that was a thing!

The phone calls I received were never from sweet Grandma Lily inviting me over to lunch. In fact, for many parents such as I, phone calls herald a no-nonsense voice announcing that my child was arrested for stealing or was found unconscious on the floor due to a drug overdose. It may be a call from school saying my child was involved in a bullying incident or is in the counselor's office because they made suicidal comments. Maybe it is a call from the program director saying I missed my monthly payment due to a lack of funds in my account. A phone call may bring news that I'm about to lose our home or expose crisis in my marriage because of my hurting child.

I always worried that, when the phone rang it would be the dreaded call from my husband telling me to get home because our daughter went over the top in doing something crazy, precipitating a heated argument. I worried when a call from our church leader said that Daniela's behaviors made others uncomfortable. I worried that Daniela would dive deeper into more risky dares just to prove a five-foot, eighty-five-pound girl can do just as

know. I could give up as if to say that not even God could rescue me or I could give in and surrender my will to His will. In my dream, I surrendered and immediately felt God's presence and peace.

How often have we lived with no peace and allowed the flesh to torment our mind with worry when we didn't need to? I've done it many times. I have allowed worry to plague me to the point of rendering me nonfunctional, leaving no room for God to minister to me or my child.

Finding God's peace for our families only happens through prayer, giving thanks, and spending time in God's Word. We must be vigilant to guard our heart and mind against the enemy who wants to tear down our hope, our faith, and our trust.

This will not be easy. Yet, God's Word encourages us in Psalm 55:22 NIV, *"Cast your cares on the LORD and he will sustain you; he will never let the righteous be shaken."*

The next time you hear a little voice saying, "It's time to get worried," respond with this: "It's time to pray, praise, give thanks, and lay all my worries at His feet." When you fall to your knees in prayer, you will rise with less anxiety weighing you down. Let the Lord carry your cares and worries. He already knows the outcome of each woe and how to minister to your family through it all.

Go Deeper

 How can you change your everyday worry into an everyday trust and faith in God?

 How can you apply the three things you need in Philippians 4:6 so you will be worry free?

 Worrying is the opposite of God's character. In essence, when we worry, we are saying that we cannot trust God who sees all and knows all. By laying down our worry, what are we proclaiming to God?

Meditate on Scripture

Worry weighs a person down; an encouraging word cheers a person up.

Proverbs 12:25 NLT

Can any one of you by worrying add a single hour to your life?

Matthew 6:27 NIV

Now may the Lord of peace himself give you peace at all times and in every way. The Lord be with all of you.

2 Thessalonians 3:16 NIV

Pray

Dear Heavenly Father,

You have provided peace in place of worry. You know worry weighs me down. Forgive me for not leaning on

Your promises and Word when I am fearful and troubled. I cannot find peace in the world. It only comes from You. When I ask for peace, I know You will give it to me. When an issue arises and I don't know how to respond, help me call upon the Holy Spirit to empower me as I pray and read Your Word. Remove all my anxiety, doubts, and fears, and replace them with encouragement, peace, and a cheerful heart. May I not take them back and burden myself again. Lord Jesus may Your peacefulness, calm spirit, and confidence reside within me as I meet You humbly at the cross and lay my burdens down.

Amen

"We fail in the work of
grace and love
when there is too much of us
and not enough of God."

— Suzanne Woods Fisher

Afterword
A Final Word of Encouragement

Our journey as parents continues into the young adulthood of our children. Once a parent, always a parent. We will have highs and lows; see victories and failures. We will wonder if God hears our prayers. We will also be amazed at the way God responds to those prayers.

The number of times I cried my eyes out, God must have used a football-field-sized pool to store up all my tears because a bottle would not be big enough. Somewhere in the midst of grieving over my broken child, I gave up doing it my way.

This became true of us as a family when we tried to weather the storms each in our own way, finding only that each way often conflicted one with another. Turbulent waves knocked us off our feet and dragged us into dangerous current tides every time. Our own way didn't work. We all had to let go and let God take over. To be honest, it was the best decision we ever made as individuals—and as a family.

The only way we survived our parenting storms was

to sink our anchor deep into prayer and the Word of God. When we finally submitted to God in obedience and allowed Him to begin the work of releasing us from our emotional bondage, our tempest storms calmed. We settled into a place of peace that we had not known before—at least not for a very long time. This did not mean that our daughter's battles disappeared. In fact, she still struggled through them to some degree. But sheltered in a new place of understanding and God's love for her, she grew in the knowledge that the Lord wanted to heal her His way.

In our sailing the turbulent seas of life as hurting parents, we discovered it is not good to be alone. In fact, we found that we needed to be rescued quite often by supportive co-believers and other kindred parents who understood the pain and confusion of torn mainsails and damaged rudders that capsize boats in a storm. If we didn't call out for help with a hearty, "Mayday!" alert, we surely would have drowned. I am so thankful that God sent those beloved ones to come alongside us in our distress.

Rescued from drowning, the Lord continued to work His deliverance in our lives. I needed healing. My husband needed healing. Lots. Of. It. God used our brokenness as an example for Daniela to see how she was not the only one suffering. Her parents struggled with pain in their lives, too. Over time, I shared my emotional turmoil with her, explaining how carrying such burdens for so many years could not restore me. Only with God's healing power of liberation and deliverance, and strong Scriptural counsel, did I see my shattered heart become whole again.

God is a miracle working God and can calm any storm. *"Then they cried to the LORD in their trouble, And He brought them out of their distresses. He caused the storm to be still so that the waves of the sea were hushed. Then they were glad because they were quiet, So He guided them to their desired haven . . . "* Psalm 107:28-30 NASB. If we do not keep our focus on Him, we too, will falter and find ourselves sinking into the dark depths of hopelessness.

Our Lord provides great promises for families that wholly trust Him to be true to each of these promises in Jesus Christ. Learn and walk in this simple truth: Rely on His faithfulness no matter how bad the storm rages and swirls about you.

Make the Word of God and intercessory prayer the two key elements built firmly into your foundation as you navigate your way on this challenging journey. I have relied on the Word to get me through our family's toughest times and have prayed the deepest of prayers while enduring excruciating, emotional turmoil and suffering through affliction and trials. Jesus was my anchor during these tsunami struggles of parenting and continues to be so.

May you find your Anchor in Jesus, too. He has promised to lead you through the storms of life with your teen. May you find strength and courage day by day knowing His grace is truly sufficient.

RESOURCES

God is our Great Physician, our Mighty Counselor, and the ONLY professional in whom we can fully trust. Yet, He can also use others to support and help us too. Hurting parent—you are not alone. God is with you every step of the way and He is always at work, whether we see His hand in it or not. Prayer from faith-filled friends, support of family, and wisdom and guidance from our pastor has proven the most helpful in this journey through the turbulent waves of life with a troubled teen. They have guided and encouraged my family through some heavy storms. In addition, we discovered a host of helpful resources and support groups in addition to a strong biblical counselor, all of which have greatly benefited our family.

Books

You Are Not Alone: Hope for Hurting Parents of Troubled Kids, by Dena Yohe—Dena and her husband Tom share the story of their once out-of-control daughter Renee when she struggled with addiction, self-harm, depression, and destructive choices. Their story will leave you encouraged knowing you are not alone in your journey.

Candid Confessions of An Imperfect Parent, by Jonathan McKee—Creator of TheSource4Parents.com, has helped thousands of parents understand the rapidly changing world of youth culture while providing practical parenting tips and helps along the way.

Purging your House: Pruning your Family Tree, by Perry Stone—If you want to really change your home situation and get rid of conflict, dissatisfaction, and disillusionment, then this is the book for you. It is powerful, causing you to look deeper, on a spiritual level, in rescuing your family.

Comforting Teens in Crisis, by Group Publishing—a book for church counselors, youth leaders and helpers focusing on tough subjects while working with teens.

Prayers for Prodigals: 90 Days of Prayer for Your Child, by James Bank—Here's a wonderful book offering encouragement and strength as you pray for your prodigal child who has strayed. This book gives you the words, often difficult to say, that become prayer and words of faith. www.jamesbanks.org/books

When Your Teen Is Struggling: Real Hope and Practical Help for Parents Today, by Mark Gregston—*Heartlight* founder and executive director of a residential counseling center for teens, Mark has helped over 2,500 struggling adolescents and hosts *Parenting Today's Teens* radio program.

A Parent's Guide to Helping Teenagers in Crisis, by Rich Van Pelt, Jim Hancock—Youth pastors who have served many years in ministry dealing with teens in crisis share their expert advice and insights into the world of teens and how to get them the help they need.

Just Keep Going: Spiritual Encouragement from the Mom of a Troubled Teen, by Sarah Nielsen—A 75-day devotional with stories about a mom's love and prayer for her son who struggled with addiction.

Hope and Healing for Kids Who Cut: Learning to Understand and Help Those Who Self-Injure, by Marv Penner—This book will help the parent understand what self-harm is and is not as well as give tools to equip the parent to guide their child to healing.

Treatment Programs

Teen Challenge
www.teenchallengeusa.com
Teen Challenge (also known as Adult & Teen Challenge) is a Christ-centered Holistic approach to Drug and Alcohol Addiction offering various programs with mentoring, discipleship, personal, and group studies. They have obtained a high success rate in conquering addiction with Jesus as the foundation of their program.

Lighthouse Solutions
www.lighthousesolutions.us
A Lighthouse with Healthcare Solutions is a "single-point contact" that provides no cost, confidential assistance to

those struggling with drug and alcohol addictions, eating disorders, mood, anxiety and stress disorders, sexual addictions, gambling and other life-controlling behaviors.

Timberline Knolls
www.timberlineknolls.com
Timberline Knolls is a treatment center for women only. They mainly focus on eating disorders, drug and alcohol addictions, depression, mood and anxiety disorders, trauma and PTSD issues.

Covenant Hills Treatment Center
www.covenanthillstreatment.com
Covenant Hills is a treatment center for drug and alcohol addictions. They also specialize in co-occurring disorders and working with the Christian and traditional 12-step programs.

Compass Rose Academy
www.compassroseacademy.org
Compass Rose Academy is a prevention service and residential treatment center for troubled teens. Compass Rose Academy's Philosophy of care and growth model is based on the work of psychologist and author Dr. John Townsend, Ph. D.

Mercy Multiplied
www.mercymultiplied.com
Mercy Multiplied is a residential program that serves young women from ages 13 to 28, who struggle with eating disorders, self-harm, drug and alcohol addictions,

depression, and unplanned pregnancy. They also serve young victims of physical and sexual abuse, including sex trafficking.

Websites

Anchor of Promise
www.AnchorOfPromise.com
Stacy Lee Flury provides this support and educational blog for parents with teens/young adults in crisis.

Hope for Hurting Parents
www.HopeforHurtingParents.com
A support website for parents who are hurting over their children's choices and lifestyles.

Hurting Moms, Mending Hearts
www.hurtingmoms.com
Online community and workbook course of ten weeks to help moms unload, be encouraged, and find peace in the midst of their storms.

Door of Hope 4Teens
www.doorofhope4teens.org
Ministry for families whose children self-harm.

Teenology by TeenSafe
www.teensafe.com
This is a great resource page for parents to keep an eye on their teen's cell phone usage. It shows you how to keep your kids safe, how to uncover hidden apps, and great

videos to show your teen the dangers of the improper use of cell phones and chat apps.

National Alliance on Mental Illness
www.NAMI.org

Eating Disorder Referral
www.edreferral.com
Need support or a treatment center and don't know where to start? This site does all the searching for you by insurance, your local area, faith-based centers, and more.

Movies

In the Mirror Dimly, by Barbara Sundstrom
Cross Wind Productions
Based on the true story, a young teen battles bulimia and must face the truth of her illness while visiting her father's farm.

To Write Love on Her Arms
www.TWLOHA.com
The true story of Renee Yohe, who embarked on a journey of recovery and healing from addition and abuse. She is the daughter of Dena Yohe, author of *You Art Not Alone*.

A Word About Depression in Parents

Teens in crisis can have a tremendous effect on the mental, physical, emotional, and spiritual state of the parent. With overwhelming amounts of stress and emotional upheaval in the home, depression may result.

This was the case for me. I had no idea that I was suffering from Chronic Depression until I began my counseling sessions. In fact, I laughed at the idea because I believed depression was something other people had a problem with, not me. However, I learned that I didn't know I had depression because I did not recognize the symptoms:

- I withdrew myself from others.
- My weight plummeted to 95 pounds.
- I had trouble concentrating,
- I had no energy, was often too tired to get out of bed, and endured many sleepless nights.
- Everything bothered me.
- I felt like a failure and was extremely critical of myself.
- I was disappointed in myself, felt ashamed and guilty, blaming myself for everything.
- I wouldn't allow myself to be happy or enjoy things or former passions in life.
- I lacked any hope of a future for my family or myself.
- I thought a lot about suicide.
- Some days I'd cry and cry.
- Some days I felt dead inside.
- I couldn't make decisions anymore.
- I didn't care about how I looked.
- I thought I deserved to be this way.
- I couldn't show love or open my heart to anyone.
- I found no solace in substances—I just wanted to

give up.

- I wasn't sure if God cared about me so I stopped caring about God.
- I didn't pray anymore.
- I didn't read my Bible.
- My faith was non-existent.
- My hope was lost.

Until . . .

I walked into a counselor's office and sat down. Once I recognized all these symptoms, I could admit that I was depressed. This relieved me because now I understood why I felt as I did. The Lord did the rest. He used my counselor to break open the doors that had been locked for so long in depression. I thought I wasn't redeemable, or worthy to be rescued from the heaviness upon me. God showed me otherwise.

He can show you too. There is nothing to be ashamed of. God will meet you right where you are now, even in your depression. There is help. There is hope. The Lord has gifted many trained counselors and mental health professionals to guide us through times of extreme hopelessness. If you find yourself agreeing with any of these symptoms of depression I experienced, seek counsel now. Don't delay.

It will make a world of difference not only for your life, but that of your family too.

Special Thanks

My Lord and Savior—Five years ago, Lord, You gave me three dreams within three nights regarding this devotional. Since then, and through every high and low moment, and there were many of them, You remained faithful in seeing this devotional through to completion. I didn't fully understand what type of book, or books, I would write. However, You continued to confirm, over and over, through Your Word, others, and in counsel, that this book was part of Your plan. Yes, all good things work together for Your good and Your glory!

Marlene Bagnull—Words cannot express my gratitude for the support you showered upon me in making sure I attended the Greater Philadelphia Christian Writers Conferences, helping me to be a better writer. You told me to never give up because thousands of broken moms and dads with teens in crisis need to be encouraged and given hope. Thank you for having faith in me and the investment of your personal time and experience towards this publication.

Meg Shepherd—You have been a cherished friend of over twenty-plus years. Thank you for that extra editing help you lent, and for you and your family who prayed for me throughout this journey. I look forward to reading your upcoming novel that I know will truly hit home to the wounded souls hurt by the occult.

Scott and Kari Schneider—Dan and I have been so thankful that God put you into our lives. You understood the struggles connected with being a parent of teens in crisis. Your input, shoulder to cry on, open home, committed friendship, and prayers, is what has kept us going. And thank you, Kari, for both selling and finding us a home. You're the best!

Dena Yohe—Without your daily Scriptures from God's Word via text, I would have surely felt so alone and hopeless. You completely understood what it meant to be a parent of a teen/young adult in crisis. Thank you for your listening ear, your prayers and blog re-posts. We are on a mission to help parents across the world!

Ruth Nyce and Debbie Ferry—Your words of uplifting encouragement, kindness, and deep hearted prayers for my well-being goes beyond the calling of co-labor buddies. It was and still is a pleasure to work side by side with you both. Ruth—a big thank you for your beautiful photographic cover for this book. You are so gifted!

Deborah Cohen and Jennie Prewitt—We have prayed through a lot together. We have hurt a lot together. We opened the doors of vulnerability, sharing our hearts bare as prayer moms. I appreciated all the face time and honesty to let go of the pain and hold onto the God's Word and the hope He has given us. You guys rock!

Cynthia Griffin, My Counselor—I came into your office at 95 pounds and chronically depressed, struggling with emotional pain and hurt, as well as a tremendous amount of trauma that I had never dealt with from my past. Through our counseling sessions I was able to see and let go of the chains that held me for so long. Your guidance and prayers, plus encouragement for me to write out my emotions, produced my first written piece on depression—and eventually this book. I am forever grateful for all you've done for me. Thank you from the bottom of my heart.

Julie Wegryn, Daniela's Counselor—I knew right away that you were the one Daniela needed when she talked to you the very first time. She walked out of your office and said, "I want to see her again." It was a match made in heaven—literally! You made my job as a parent a lot easier by taking on the many crises that she carried and was going through. You laughed, you prayed, and you were always amazed at the unbelievable stories she shared every time you saw her. But underneath it all, you saw an extremely broken child who needed to be rescued. Thank you for all that you have done, especially for me.

Tom and Arlene Finnerty—Mom and Dad, what can I really say? You have been my support in so many ways and never gave up on me and my writing. You cheered for me many times and followed God's heart to see me complete this book from beginning to end. Thank you for everything!

Vicki Palaganas—Many thanks for your constant encouragement, your editing helps to point me in the right direction, prayer support, and most of all, your friendship.

Prayer Team—My heart is touched and so thankful for my prayer warrior team. You have been a constant support in praying for me, and this devotional, from the start. I felt comforted knowing that sisters and brothers in the Lord were covering me in prayer through every attack that came against the publishing of this book. I am amazed to see God move, opening doors to share this devotional with so many hurting parents who need healing. Words do not seem adequate to thank you all for praying this devotional to fruition. May God continue to be glorified and may He bless you richly in return.

Pastor Bill and Mary Brendal—You have been our rock since we stepped into Glad Tidings Church. Your commitment to be there for us in the bad and good times has humbled us greatly. Mercy, grace, compassion, and most importantly, your prayers for our family, has been evident. The Word of God flows through you Pastor Bill, and has ministered to us many times as parents, as well as servants for the Lord. We are so thankful to be a part of the Glad Tidings flock. We love you!

Dan-the-Man!—My husband, my friend, the one who endured so many years of heartache, scary moments, tough situations, painful, and hurting times. I am so thankful that we grew from our heartbreaking experiences and clung to each other through it all. We have cried together, rejoiced together, and prayed together. We were not perfect parents and we made tons of mistakes. However, God knew that we were the ones to love our children through their brokenness and healing. Most importantly, our marriage was tested multiple times and, thank goodness, we are together and stronger for it. All my love to you.

My Girls—Thank you for your love and allowing me space and the time to work on this devotional. Your constant faith in me to write it when I wanted to stop so many times meant the world to me. Bianca Joy and Daniela, this book is dedicated to you! You both took me on rocky roads and uncharted twist-turning paths. You helped me realize how I was a broken parent who needed God desperately. God is not finished with me yet as I still have more to learn. Thank you for your support. I pray and look forward to what is yet to come in your lives.

Kathryn Ross, My Editor and Publisher—Years ago we met at a small writer's group. Who would have thought then, in our small group, that one day you would be the editor and publisher of my book? As we connected through writers conferences and life experiences, my heart knew we were meant to work together because of your mission and the spirit you demonstrated. This book reflects our joint effort to see parents healed and set free from the emotional turbulences of life with a teen in crisis.

About the Author

Stacy Lee Flury watched in horror as her dream of raising a happy family crashed, like a storm-tossed wave on a rocky shoreline. Her teen daughter's troubles brought crisis into Stacy's home and pain to her heart. In those turbulent years, she learned to intimately know and depend on God.

After a few counseling sessions as a parent in crisis, Stacy Lee was encouraged to write down her thoughts and experiences. She experimented with blogging her difficult journey to help others, founding Anchor of Promise, an outreach mission to families battling upheaval in their homes. Since then, she has written for *Christian Blessings*, an online site for youth around the world, and has guest posted for Ruby for Women's online *RUBY Magazine*.

For over 25 years, Stacy Lee has served the Lord in various church ministries, from VBS, to dance and mime ministry, to the 10/40 Missions Club, and Youth Group. In addition, she has taught all ages in homeschool co-op groups. She is currently active as part of the Worship Team in her church fellowship.

Stacy Lee is mother to two daughters and is now a grandmother. When not writing, she stays busy as a full-time Mimzy, enjoying her two grandchildren. She admits to keeping Bad Day Chocolate in her office drawer to take the edge off rough days, while making her home with husband Dan for 35 years, and a few furry friends—two dogs and two cats.

Turning the Tide of Emotional Turbulence: Devotions for Parents of Teens in Crisis, is Stacy Lee's first book. Learn more about her story and mission at www.AnchorOfPromise.com.

About Pageant Wagon Publishing

Book Shepherding Services

by Kathryn Ross
Pageant Wagon Publishing

Let me help you develop the book
God is calling you to write ~
From Idea to Finished Product!

A la carte and bundle services
include:
~ Monthly Consulting Sessions
~ Editing
~ Layout & Design
~ Print Publishing
~Audio Book Recording
~ Ghostwriting

Pageant Wagon Publishing provides editing and indie publishing
services for Christian writers, and biblically based storybooks,
homeschool enrichment, and devotional works to promote a
Family Literacy Lifestyle through Christian discipleship.

Visit us online to order books
and learn more: www.pageantwagonpublishing.com

Made in the
USA
Lexington, KY